AF619236

SHAUNA YOUNG

The Homemade Transformation

Building a Life from Scratch

HOMEMADE CAKE
PUBLISHING

First published by Homemade Cake 2026

First edition

ISBN: 979-8-234-02671-2

Editing by Kamera Walton

This book was professionally typeset on Reedsy.
Find out more at reedsy.com

To my siblings,

Even during the years we were separated by silence and distance, my love for you never left me. That love carried me through the hardest seasons of my life and gave me a reason to keep moving forward when everything felt uncertain. So much of this journey was fueled by the hope that one day we would find our way back to each other.

Cheers to us!

Acknowledgments

First, I thank God for carrying me through every season of my life. Even when I could not see the path clearly, His grace guided my steps and gave me the strength to keep going.

To my siblings, thank you for finding your way back to me. Our reconnection has been one of the greatest gifts of my life.

To Diane, thank you for seeing something in me during one of the lowest seasons of my life. Your generosity, wisdom, and belief in my musical growth helped restore something in me that I thought I had lost.

To the teachers, mentors, coworkers, and friends who showed kindness along the way, your encouragement mattered more than you probably realize.

To the communities that shaped me from the music rooms in New York to the hospitals and classrooms that challenged me to grow, each experience helped form the woman I have become.

And finally, to the readers, thank you for taking the time to walk through this story with me. If any part of my journey reminds you that transformation is possible, then sharing it was worth it.

Prologue

The Night Everything Felt Lost

There was a night in California when I slept in the backseat of my car and wondered if my life had quietly fallen apart.

The parking lot was dim, the kind of place people pass through without really noticing. I remember staring at the ceiling of my car, listening to the distant sound of traffic and trying to convince myself that everything would eventually make sense.

My entire life was packed into that vehicle.

Clothes in the trunk.

A few notebooks filled with song lyrics.

Makeup bags.

Stage outfits from performances that once made me feel powerful.

But that night I didn't feel powerful.

I felt tired.

Not the kind of tired sleep fixes.

The kind that settles deep in your spirit after years of trying to build something that keeps collapsing.

I had chased music across cities.

Worked in record label offices.

Performed on stages.

Lived in apartments I could barely afford.

Loved people who did not love me back.

Believed in opportunities that never arrived.

And now I was here.

Thirty dollars in my account.

Sleeping in my car.

Trying to figure out how a life full of dreams had turned into survival.

But what I didn't know that night was this:

That parking lot was not the end of my story.

It was the beginning of my transformation.

Because the woman writing these words today is not the same woman who fell asleep in that car.

And the journey between those two versions of me is the story you are about to read.

1

California Love

Some people grow up knowing exactly where they belong.

Their childhood has a single setting. One hometown. One set of familiar streets. One place that always feels like home.

That was never my story.

My life began in California, under a sky so blue it almost felt endless. But the memories that shaped me unfolded thousands of miles away in Connecticut, beneath clouds that seemed to linger longer than they should.

Two coasts.

Two climates.

Two completely different worlds.

And somewhere in between them was me, a child trying to

understand how life could change so suddenly without anyone fully explaining why.

When people ask me where I'm from, the answer has never felt simple.

Because the truth is, my life began in one place, but the person I would eventually become was shaped somewhere else entirely.

My parents met in Los Angeles at church.

My mother was singing in the choir that day. She had a voice that could quiet a room, the kind of voice that made people pause mid conversation and turn their heads toward the sound. In the church community back in Hartford, Connecticut, where she was originally from, people already knew her for that voice. She was respected for it. Celebrated for it. At one point she had even sung the national anthem at NBA games.

Singing did not make her nervous.

It made her alive.

My father noticed her immediately.

He saw something in her that day standing in that choir loft. Confidence. Grace. Presence. The kind of presence that comes from someone who understands the power of their own voice.

That was how their story began.

What most people never knew about my beginning was that my

parents struggled to have children. I was not conceived naturally. I was conceived through artificial insemination, something that required both hope and faith from them at the time.

Before I ever took my first breath, I was already a child born through intention.

Through prayer.

Through effort.

I was their miracle.

But miracles do not always guarantee a perfect story.

My parents divorced when I was about one year old. I do not remember them together. There are no images in my mind of them sitting at the same table or walking side by side as a couple.

Those memories simply do not exist.

What I do remember, however, is something strangely tender considering the circumstances.

They used to communicate through letters.

Those letters traveled back and forth inside my backpack.

My father would write one.

My mother would respond.

And somehow, in the middle of their separation, those folded pieces of paper became their way of speaking to each other through me.

Even now, when I think about it, there is something bittersweet about that image. Two adults trying to navigate distance, responsibility, and parenthood through handwritten messages carried by a small child who did not yet understand what any of it meant.

I was five years old when we moved to Connecticut.

At that age, you do not fully understand divorce. You do not understand adult decisions or broken relationships. You only feel the shift.

One day your world feels whole.

And the next it has been rearranged in ways no one really explains to you.

My father stayed behind in California.

My mother packed up our lives and moved us across the country to Connecticut, back to her hometown, where she believed we could start over.

She would eventually remarry there.

But for me, the move did not feel like a fresh start.

It felt like something had been taken.

At first, there was an arrangement that helped bridge the distance between California and Connecticut. I would travel back to California alone to visit my father.

Looking back now, it seems almost unbelievable that such a young child could fly across the country alone. But that was how it worked back then. My mother would walk me through the airport and place me into the care of a flight attendant. I would be escorted onto the plane like a tiny VIP.

I remember feeling important.

Almost like a celebrity.

The stewardess would check on me throughout the flight, making sure I had snacks, juice, and something to keep me entertained. I would sit tall in my seat, staring out the window as the plane lifted into the sky.

From above, the clouds looked soft enough to land on.

Like giant pillows floating beneath us.

I loved those flights.

They felt like small adventures.

But they also carried something deeper.

They carried hope.

Hope that distance did not have to mean separation.

Hope that the life I remembered in California still existed somewhere waiting for me.

When the plane landed, my father would be there.

Waiting.

From what I remember, my time with him always felt like magic compressed into a short visit. Disneyland was almost guaranteed. He would pack us a lunch, and we would climb into his old red Corvette.

I can still see it in flashes.

The shine of it.

The way the sunlight bounced off the hood.

The wind rushing past us when he drove.

The music playing through the speakers as we moved through the California streets.

For those moments, nothing felt broken.

Those visits became small islands of joy in my childhood. I looked forward to them the way children count down the days until Christmas. They were brief, but they carried the warmth of a life that once felt whole.

But those visits did not last forever.

I was around ten years old when they stopped.

All I remember is my mother telling me to tell him I had missed my flight.

And that was the end of it.

There was no final conversation that I can recall. No dramatic goodbye. Just an absence that quietly settled into my life and never really left.

Looking back now, it amazes me how something so life altering can happen with so little explanation.

One day those trips existed.

And the next they did not.

And life simply continued.

I was not happy about moving to Connecticut.

In fact, I was devastated.

Gone were the familiar streets.

Gone were the friends I had started to make.

Gone was my father and the warmth that only California sunshine can give you.

Connecticut felt colder.

Not just in temperature, but in atmosphere.

The skies seemed gray more often than blue, and slowly my spirit began to match that color.

My world became smaller.

More sheltered.

And so did my voice.

After we moved, my mother had three children with my stepfather. He was a hardworking man who spent long hours trying to provide for our family. At the time, I could not fully understand the pressure he carried. Supporting four children was no small responsibility, and he did everything he could to keep our household afloat.

I respect that now in a way I could not understand then.

Every morning before we woke up, my mother would drive him to work. She left early while the sky was still dark. She would return briefly and then leave again for most of the day.

Survival required movement.

It required effort.

It required sacrifice.

That meant I was often left at home with my siblings.

They would sit in front of the television for hours, absorbed in whatever show was playing. The house would feel still, quiet except for the hum of cartoons and commercials echoing through the living room.

I did something different.

I listened to music.

While they watched television, I put on headphones or turned the radio up just enough to disappear into it. Music filled the space that silence created. It felt like company. It felt like understanding.

Songs became my escape.

They became the soundtrack to long afternoons and quiet evenings.

Around that same time, something happened in my life that would shape my path in ways I could not understand then.

After the sixth grade, I stopped attending school.

There was no official plan for homeschooling. There were no lesson schedules or structured classes waiting at the kitchen table. My mother was navigating poverty, survival, and responsibilities that often felt overwhelming.

Preparing for school each day required stability.

Transportation.

Paperwork.

Clean clothes.

Predictability.

Those things were not always consistent in our home.

I do not believe my mother's intention was to limit me. I believe she was doing the best she could with what she had.

But what began as disruption slowly became isolation.

Without classmates.

Without daily interaction.

Without the natural friction of growing up around peers.

I folded inward.

There were no lockers.

No hallway noise.

No cafeteria tables filled with laughter.

No dances.

No awkward middle school milestones.

There was just home.

And church.

Faith wrapped tightly around my upbringing. Both my grandparents and my great grandparents were pastors. They led their own congregations, New Hope Church of God in Christ and Victory Temple Church of God in Christ.

Church was not optional.

It was identity.

It was structure.

It was community.

As the granddaughter of church leaders, there were expectations. One of them was participating in service. Not just attending, but standing before the entire congregation to offer a sermonic solo.

It was tradition.

A moment of worship.

A family honor.

For me, it was pure terror.

I loved music with a passion so deep it almost hurt. Songs made me feel understood in a way people did not. Music gave language to emotions I could not explain.

But there was another layer to that pressure.

My mother was a singer.

And not just any singer.

People in the church community knew her voice. They admired it. They celebrated it. Because of that, people expected something from me too.

They assumed I would sing like her.

They expected me to carry the same confidence she had.

That expectation followed me everywhere.

When I sang alone, I felt free.

But standing in front of a sea of expectant eyes, holding a microphone with trembling hands, I could barely breathe.

My palms would sweat.

My heart would race.

The same girl who loved music in private could not reconcile that love with performing in public.

My shyness did not match the size of my dreams.

And it was not just church.

I was the girl who stayed tucked into the background. Too shy to lift my eyes when the boys I secretly liked were nearby. I would replay conversations in my mind at night, crafting the perfect responses.

Imagining confidence.

Imagining ease.

But when the moment came, when they were actually standing in front of me, the words always got stuck somewhere between my heart and my mouth.

Instead, I would smile.

A small, nervous smile.

And let the moment slip away.

At night, when the house was quiet and the world felt less

intimidating, I became someone else in my imagination.

I would call the local radio station and request songs like *Dangerously in Love* by Destiny's Child or *Dreaming of You* by Selena.

As the music played through the speakers in my dark room, I would imagine a different version of myself.

One who was bold enough to tell people how she felt.

One who was not trapped behind walls of fear.

One who could sing without trembling and speak without shrinking.

Inside me, there was a wildfire.

A longing to be seen.

To be heard.

To become something more than the shy girl with a big dream tucked into her chest like a secret.

Music was my refuge.

It filled the silence of long days at home.

It softened the ache of distance.

It gave language to emotions I did not yet have the courage to speak out loud.

I may not have had a classroom.

I may not have had confidence.

I may not have had the stability other children seemed to move through so effortlessly.

But I had sound.

I had imagination.

I had a voice, even if it trembled.

And somewhere between church solos, quiet bedrooms, and late night radio requests, something was forming inside of me.

I did not know it then, but the shy girl who was afraid to speak was slowly learning how to listen.

And that would change everything.

* * *

2

Different Route

Before I ever stood behind a microphone or stepped into a recording studio, music was my sanctuary.

Long before I had the language to explain my emotions, I sang them.

I would sneak into the bathroom, shut the door, and hum into the echo of tile and running water. The acoustics made my voice sound bigger than I felt. Fuller. Braver.

The bathroom became my rehearsal room.

My hiding place.

The one place in the house where I could experiment with my voice without feeling exposed. The sound of running water masked my nerves, and the echo of the walls gave me the illusion that I belonged somewhere larger than that small room.

I sang everything.

Gospel songs from church.

R&B ballads that played on the radio.

Pop melodies that floated through the airwaves late at night.

Sometimes I did not even realize I was singing. The melodies simply rose up from somewhere inside me, like breath.

Music was the one place where my emotions made sense.

But by fourteen, something else had begun growing inside me.

Restlessness.

A quiet but persistent feeling that my life was supposed to be moving forward, even though everything around me seemed frozen.

I did not go to high school.

After sixth grade, my mother stopped enrolling me in school. We were deeply poor, and survival came before structure. There were bills. Responsibilities. Realities that do not pause just because a child needs a classroom.

She never explained it fully, but I understood enough to know we were surviving, not thriving.

I do not fault her.

She did the best she could with what she had.

Still, at fourteen, something inside me refused to accept that my education had simply ended.

I wanted more.

That was when I started riding the bus alone to downtown Hartford.

At first, it felt intimidating.

I was just a young girl navigating the city by herself, but the moment I stepped onto that bus, something inside me shifted.

The bus felt like freedom.

I would sit by the window and watch the city pass by, imagining a life that felt larger than the one I was living. Storefronts opened for the day. People rushed to jobs. Students walked down the sidewalks with backpacks slung over their shoulders.

Everyone seemed to be going somewhere.

And for the first time, I was too.

My destination was always the same.

The library.

If I did not have a traditional classroom, I would build my own.

I walked through those doors like they belonged to me. The quiet hum of people studying. The smell of books and paper. The rows of shelves stretching in every direction.

Possibility lived there.

I remember running my fingers across the spines of books as if I were choosing doors to walk through.

And I read everything.

Fiction.

Nonfiction.

Biographies.

Self-help books.

Anything that expanded my thinking beyond the walls of our apartment.

Sometimes I would lose track of time completely. Hours would pass while I sat at the same wooden table, turning page after page.

The library became my school.

It became my discipline.

It became my quiet rebellion against the idea that my education had stopped.

While my siblings stayed home watching television, I was downtown reading and imagining a life that stretched far beyond the circumstances I had been born into.

I did not realize it then, but those hours in the library were shaping the way I would think for the rest of my life.

I was learning how to teach myself.

Around that same time, I began visiting my cousin at her job at a local dental office.

I was fourteen.

Sometimes I would take the bus just to see her and sit quietly in the waiting room, observing how everything worked.

I watched patients check in.

I watched the receptionist answer phones with calm professionalism.

I watched the rhythm of the office.

People arrived with problems and left with solutions.

Everything moved with purpose.

Something about that environment fascinated me.

Everyone had a role.

Everyone knew what they were responsible for.

It felt structured in a way my life did not.

One day, the dentist noticed me sitting there.

He asked my cousin about me and then came over to introduce himself.

After a short conversation, he told me something that surprised me.

"I love your smile," he said.

He told me it was warm. Inviting.

He said people who called the office would be able to hear me smiling through the phone.

I was shy, but I smiled even harder when he said that.

Then he offered me a job.

At fourteen years old, I became a receptionist at a dental office.

It was my first real responsibility.

I answered phones.

Scheduled appointments.

Greeted patients when they walked through the door.

I learned how to speak clearly and professionally. I learned how to look people in the eye and communicate confidently, even when I still felt uncertain inside.

That office taught me something important.

How to present myself to the world.

But it also became the beginning of something much harder.

When I started earning money, I felt proud.

It was not much, but it was mine.

My first paychecks made me feel grown in a way I had never experienced before.

Soon, my mother began asking me for money.

At first it seemed small.

But quickly it became everything.

Not a little here and there.

My entire paycheck.

At fourteen, I did not have the language to explain why that felt wrong. I just knew something inside me felt stretched thin.

I was working.

But I had nothing to show for it.

The pride I felt when I first started earning money slowly turned into frustration.

One day, overwhelmed and confused, I ran to my cousin's house and told her everything.

She listened quietly.

She did not interrupt.

She just let me talk.

When I finished, she asked me a question that caught me completely off guard.

"Are you even enrolled in school?"

I paused.

I had never thought about the question that way before.

No.

I wasn't.

She looked at me carefully and said something that would change the course of my life.

"You need to call your father and tell him the truth."

So I did.

I picked up the phone and told him everything.

About not being in school.

About giving my paychecks away.

About how confused I felt.

He listened quietly.

Then he gave me advice that felt enormous for someone my age.

He told me to call the police.

At fourteen years old, I made a decision no child should have to make.

I called.

The police came to my cousin's house. They spoke with me briefly and then contacted my mother, asking her to come pick me up.

When she arrived, something happened that shocked me.

She told the officers that I was emotionally unstable.

And then she said something that left me completely stunned.

She claimed that my father had molested me.

That was not true.

Nothing like that had ever happened.

Hearing that accusation felt like the air had been knocked out of my lungs.

I did not understand why she would say that.

I just remember standing there feeling confused.

Small.

Powerless.

After that, I went back home.

But something inside me had shifted permanently.

Trust had cracked.

Life continued, but it was never quite the same again.

By the time I was sixteen, the restlessness inside me had turned into determination.

Somewhere during that season, I saw a flyer about the GED test.

I was still a minor.

But I wanted a chance.

So I forged my mother's signature and signed up.

The first time I took the test, I failed.

I remember walking away feeling disappointed, but not defeated.

For the first time in my life, I had stepped toward something on my own.

Even in failing, I felt movement.

So I studied harder.

I returned to the library.

The same place that had quietly educated me for years.

I read more.

Practiced more.

Prepared more.

At sixteen, going on seventeen, I took the test again.

This time, I passed.

I remember holding the letter in my hands and reading it over and over again just to make sure it was real.

It was one of the first times I felt deeply proud of myself.

Like I had opened a door that no one expected me to walk through.

Around that same time, my mom often shopped at a local grocery store where I met Ricky.

He was Puerto Rican, quiet, and polite in a way that immediately stood out to me.

He had great manners.

He was not loud or flashy.

He carried himself with a calm confidence that felt steady.

He lived with his mom and two sisters in a nice neighborhood.

Their home felt structured.

Stable.

Very different from the instability I had grown used to.

He had a car.

And whenever he picked me up, the speakers were usually blasting reggaeton. The bass vibrated through the seats while the music pulsed through the car.

I would sit there smiling, pretending I was not secretly nervous.

That music was different from what I listened to alone in my room.

It was bold.

Rhythmic.

Full of life.

Ricky himself was gentle.

Soft spoken.

Respectful.

The music would be loud, but he was not.

He opened doors.

He spoke kindly.

He never made me feel rushed or pressured.

For a girl who had spent years shrinking into the background, that mattered more than I realized at the time.

When we drove through his neighborhood with the music turned up, I felt like I was stepping into another world.

A world where things seemed possible.

My mom, surprisingly, played matchmaker.

She liked him.

Trusted him.

We dated for over a year.

He took me out to eat.

To movies.

Sometimes we would just drive around the city for hours.

I remember sitting in the passenger seat, watching the streets pass by through the window, feeling like life was slowly widening in front of me.

Even though I never walked a traditional high school hallway, I still got to wear the dress.

At seventeen, I went to his junior prom.

I remember the lights.

The music.

The way the room buzzed with teenage energy.

Students laughing.

Dancing.

Taking pictures.

I felt both out of place and exactly where I was meant to be.

For one night, I was not the girl who stayed home.

I even took the SAT alongside him.

Sitting in that classroom with a number two pencil, filling in bubbles on the test sheet, I felt something shift inside me.

I was not defined by the classrooms I had never stepped into.

I was not limited to the version of myself that circumstances had tried to shrink.

Music was still my secret.

But at sixteen and seventeen, I began to understand something important.

Truth has a cost.

Independence has a cost.

And sometimes doing the right thing makes you lonely.

But I was not behind.

I was just on a different route.

And the fact that I was moving at all meant I was not stuck.

For the first time in my life, I believed something powerful.

Even if my beginning looked unconventional...

My future did not have to.

* * *

WICKED

3

One Way to Chicago

In our family, Sundays were sacred.

Church was not just a ritual. It was the heartbeat of our week, a place where appearances mattered and roles were assigned early. I sang in the choir, smiled when expected, and played the part of the dutiful daughter and granddaughter.

On the outside, everything looked orderly.

Respectable.

Faithful.

But beneath the polished surface, I often felt invisible.

Like a background character in my own life.

I had learned how to perform long before I ever stood on a stage. I knew how to show up. I knew how to say the right things and smile at the right moments. I knew how to carry myself in ways that kept everyone comfortable.

I had learned how to shrink parts of myself so the room could stay peaceful.

But there was one thing I had not learned yet.

How to choose myself.

One Sunday after service, I lingered near a group of older women chatting with a fellow choir member. They were asking her about her plans after graduation.

She mentioned applying to Columbia College in Chicago.

Columbia College.

The name stayed with me.

Something about it settled in my mind long after the conversation ended. I went home that afternoon repeating the words quietly to myself like a secret.

Columbia College.

Chicago.

The next morning I took the bus downtown to the library.

The library had already become my second home, the place

where I educated myself when traditional school was no longer part of my life. I walked straight to the computers and began researching the school.

What I discovered felt almost unbelievable.

It was a performing arts college.

A school where students studied music.

Film.

Writing.

Art.

Creativity was not just welcomed there.

It was the entire purpose.

For the first time, music felt less like a private refuge and more like a possible future.

The idea that someone could go to school to study creativity felt surreal. My heart started beating faster the more I read.

People built careers doing this.

People studied the very thing that had comforted me through some of the loneliest years of my life.

The thought both excited and terrified me.

Still, I applied.

I filled out the application with trembling confidence, not knowing what would happen next.

Weeks later, an acceptance letter arrived.

I remember standing in the kitchen holding the envelope.

My hands were shaking.

I opened it slowly and read the words over and over again just to make sure I had not misunderstood.

I had been accepted.

Someone believed I belonged there.

Someone believed I had potential.

It felt like someone had opened a door I did not even know existed.

And I was standing on the threshold.

With three hundred dollars in my pocket, I booked a one-way flight to Chicago.

It was not practical.

It was not financially secure.

It was not carefully mapped out.

But it was mine.

Leaving Connecticut felt surreal.

I packed the few things I owned into a suitcase and headed to the airport with excitement and fear swirling together inside my chest.

Part of me wondered if I was making a mistake.

Another part of me knew something even stronger.

If I did not try, I would regret it forever.

When the plane began its descent into Chicago, I pressed my forehead against the window.

The city stretched endlessly below me.

Skyscrapers rose from the earth like steel monuments. Lake Michigan shimmered beside them like an ocean.

Everything looked enormous.

Bigger than anything I had ever known.

For a moment, fear crept in.

What am I doing here?

But the plane landed anyway.

And so did I.

Arriving at Columbia College was both exhilarating and intimidating.

Families filled the dorms. Parents carried boxes through the hallways. Mothers arranged bedding and folded clothes into drawers while fathers offered advice that sounded equal parts protective and proud.

Everyone seemed to have someone there helping them settle in.

I stood alone with one suitcase.

I did not have sheets.

Or pillows.

Or toilet paper.

Or detergent.

I had thought about leaving.

About becoming.

About stepping into something bigger.

But I had not thought about the small details.

I remember sitting on the bare mattress in my dorm room staring at the blank walls.

The room echoed with quiet.

For a brief moment, doubt crept in.

Maybe I had been too bold.

Maybe I had made a mistake.

Then I reminded myself why I had come.

To become someone new.

Later that afternoon, while wandering the hallway trying to figure out where everything was, I bumped into a girl who introduced herself as Bianca from Louisville, Kentucky.

She noticed I was by myself.

She noticed I did not have much.

There was something about her energy that felt warm and immediate.

When she asked if I had everything I needed for my room, I hesitated before answering.

She did not press me.

Instead, she smiled and said something simple.

"Let's go to Target."

That small act of kindness meant everything.

Bianca became my first friend in Chicago.

She introduced me to all of her friends, and suddenly I was surrounded by a creative community that felt vibrant and alive.

She was studying film, and her life seemed to move with artistic momentum.

She invited me to film sets she was producing, and I watched as ideas slowly transformed into scenes.

Scripts became visuals.

Conversations became direction.

Lights.

Cameras.

Actors repeating lines again and again until the moment felt right.

For the first time, I saw that creativity was not just inspiration.

It was work.

It was planning.

It was collaboration.

Art was not just emotion.

It was discipline.

Bianca also introduced me to a social world I had never experienced before.

She got me an ID, and we began going out to clubs together.

The music was loud.

The lights were dim.

The rooms pulsed with energy.

Bodies moved to the rhythm of bass lines that seemed to shake the walls.

For a girl who had grown up sheltered and isolated, Chicago nightlife felt like stepping into color after years of grayscale.

Everything felt bigger.

Faster.

More alive.

I was still shy.

But I was no longer invisible.

Academically, however, I was learning quickly that passion alone was not enough.

I did not understand financial aid forms.

I did not know how to navigate deadlines or grants.

There were systems and processes that most students seemed to already understand.

I felt behind.

Overwhelmed by paperwork and unfamiliar rules.

Still, I registered for classes.

Eventually I chose to major in music.

During my first semester, I enrolled in a music production class without knowing what to expect.

There were only four other students.

Dean.

Brian.

And a married couple whose names I cannot recall.

Then the professor walked in.

Donald Lawrence.

One of the greatest songwriters in gospel music.

I remember the moment he entered the room.

The energy shifted immediately.

He carried himself with quiet authority, like someone who did not need to announce his greatness because the room already knew it.

I sat there stunned.

Donald Lawrence.

Teaching my class.

He was kind.

Observant.

Intentional.

He took me, Dean, and Brian under his wing.

Maybe he saw our hunger.

Our curiosity.

Our willingness to learn.

Sometimes he would take us out to dinner after class and talk about songwriting in a way that felt almost sacred.

He spoke about melody.

Structure.

Integrity.

Excellence.

He explained how a song was not just a collection of notes.

It was a conversation between emotion and craft.

The right chord progression could unlock something in a listener's heart that words alone could never reach.

He did not just teach music.

He taught discipline.

He taught intention.

That first semester felt intimate.

Focused.

Personal.

But at the end of the semester, reality arrived.

I was called into the Dean's office and told I had a balance due.

My heart sank.

I knew I did not have the money.

In that moment, I chose honesty.

I explained that I did not fully understand financial aid when I enrolled.

I told him I did not come from money.

I told him I was doing everything I could to stay in school.

Then I asked him for something simple.

Just let me finish the year.

Just the year.

He listened.

And he agreed.

Second semester arrived with a completely different energy.

Word had spread about the class.

The room was much larger now.

And during that semester, Donald asked me to be his teacher's aide.

Out of all the students, he chose me.

I sat beside him at the front of the classroom grading papers and observing everything.

How he corrected people with grace.

How he encouraged students without lowering his standards.

How he listened before speaking.

I learned as much from watching him as I did from the lessons themselves.

The shy girl who once trembled during church solos was now seated beside one of gospel music's most respected songwriters.

Music was no longer a secret.

It was becoming my identity.

Around that same time, something unexpected happened.

My father came to visit me in Chicago.

It was the first time I had seen him since I was ten years old.

I felt nervous.

Unsure.

When I opened the dorm room door and saw him standing there, time seemed to pause.

The first thing I noticed was the smell of alcohol on his breath.

He seemed different.

More guarded.

Looking back now, I think he was just as emotional as I was.

He simply did not know how to show it.

Our visit was short.

Just a day or two.

One evening we went to dinner together.

While we were sitting there, a woman at a nearby table struck up a conversation with us.

She complimented my father, calling him handsome, and introduced herself.

She told us she ran a nonprofit organization and was looking for interns.

It would be a paid internship.

She handed me her contact information.

I called her.

And shortly afterward, I became her intern.

Those small checks, combined with food stamps, were how I survived that year in Chicago.

They were not large amounts of money.

But they were enough.

Before my father left Chicago, he handed me a check for books.

I instantly started crying.

It was not about the money.

It was about the gesture.

It was about him showing up.

We did not unpack the past.

We did not resolve everything.

But something softened between us.

Chicago stretched me.

I had flown across the country alone.

I had survived with almost nothing.

I had studied under a respected songwriter.

I had reunited with my father.

I had worked.

I had interned.

I had stepped into spaces I once believed were unreachable.

So when I eventually packed my bags and returned to Connecticut, moving into my grandmother Etta Mae's one-bedroom apartment where her couch became my bed, it could have felt like failure.

But it did not.

Because Chicago had changed me.

Even though I returned home, I was not the same girl who left.

And deep down, I knew something important.

This was only the beginning.

* * *

4

In the Room

Returning to Connecticut after Chicago was not the end of my story.

It was an intermission.

I moved back into my grandmother Etta Mae's one-bedroom apartment. Her couch became my bed. Her small living room became my temporary world.

On paper, it may have looked like a setback.

But internally, something had shifted.

I had flown across the country alone.

I had survived.

I had studied under Donald Lawrence. I had been asked to serve as his teacher's aide during my second semester. I had reunited with my father. I had worked, interned, and stretched myself beyond fear.

Even though I was back in Connecticut, I was not the same girl who left.

Something inside me had awakened.

I had seen the world.

And now I wanted more of it.

Dean

During that season, I stayed in contact with Dean.

Dean had graduated from Columbia College Chicago. Because of his relationship with Professor Donald Lawrence, he had been introduced to A&R executive Jimmy Maynes.

That connection led to a summer internship at Jive Records in New York City.

Jive Records.

Even saying the name felt big.

The label had shaped so much of the music that filled my headphones growing up. Being anywhere near that building meant proximity to the industry I had been dreaming about for years.

While I was back in Connecticut recalibrating my next move, Dean was stepping deeper into that world.

And I was watching closely.

His birthday happened to fall near the end of his internship.

Hartford was only about three and a half hours from New York City.

I decided to hop on a Greyhound bus to visit him.

Part of me wanted to celebrate his birthday.

But another part of me wanted something else.

I wanted to see the room.

The industry room.

The room I had dreamed about but had never stood inside.

Jive Records

When I arrived in New York, Dean invited me up to the Jive Records office while he finished wrapping up a few things before we went out to eat.

I didn't mind waiting.

I sat quietly in the corner, observing everything around me.

The energy in that office felt different.

Focused.

Busy.

Intentional.

Phones rang constantly. People walked briskly through the hallways carrying folders and CDs. Conversations hummed low but strategic.

You could feel that decisions were being made in those rooms.

Decisions that could change someone's life.

This was not fantasy.

This was the machine.

I remember taking in the details. The walls. The desks. The movement. The confidence people carried when they walked past. No one seemed to be wandering. Everyone looked like they had somewhere important to be and something important to do.

That alone fascinated me.

For so long, the music industry had lived in my imagination as something shiny and far away. But sitting there in that office, I could finally see it for what it was.

Work.

Pressure.

Taste.

Timing.

Relationships.

A thousand decisions happening behind closed doors.

Then he walked in.

Jimmy Maynes.

He entered the room like electricity.

Bright personality. Unmistakable New York accent. All presence. All confidence.

The kind of person who filled a room without trying.

Dean introduced us casually.

Jimmy looked at me for a moment and smiled.

"You got good energy," he said.

That one sentence felt like permission.

Before I had time to overthink it, I asked him something bold.

"What are you going to do when Dean's internship ends?"

He shrugged.

"I don't know. I probably need another intern."

I smiled.

"Well, I'll be your next intern."

He didn't hesitate.

"Great," he said. "Start Monday."

Just like that.

No resume.

No formal interview.

Just boldness.

I should have been terrified.

Instead, I felt alive.

The kind of alive that comes from realizing one moment of courage can shift the entire direction of your life.

The Greyhound Commute

The Greyhound ride back to Connecticut that night felt surreal.

The bus windows were dark mirrors reflecting my face back at me. I stared at my reflection as the city lights blurred past.

Nineteen years old.

Broke.

But somehow in the room.

I had just landed an internship at one of the most talked-about record labels in New York.

It didn't matter that it was unpaid.

It didn't matter that I had no idea how I would afford commuting back and forth.

This was my chance.

And I was not letting it slip away.

Starting that Monday, my life became something out of a movie.

Every weekday morning, I boarded a Greyhound bus from Hartford to Penn Station.

Three hours there.

Three hours back.

Six hours of travel for maybe four hours inside the office.

I would wake up before sunrise, throw on whatever outfit made me feel the most confident, grab my bag, and head to the bus station.

The buses smelled like diesel fuel and stale coffee. Sometimes they were crowded.

Sometimes quiet.

Sometimes filled with people chasing their own opportunities.

But every single ride carried the same feeling.

Hope.

Some mornings I was exhausted before the day had even started. But I learned quickly that exhaustion feels different when it is connected to purpose. I wasn't riding those buses because I had nowhere else to go.

I was riding them because somewhere on the other side of that commute was access to the life I wanted.

Some days I didn't even have money for the bus fare.

On those mornings, I would stand outside with my backpack and my determination, explaining my situation to the driver.

Over time, they started recognizing me.

They knew my name.

Some of them knew my story.

Maybe they saw the hunger in my eyes.

Or maybe they remembered what it felt like to want something so badly you were willing to risk embarrassment just to get closer to it.

Either way, many of them let me on.

And every time I stepped onto that bus, I promised myself I would not waste the opportunity waiting on the other side.

That commute became part of my education too.

It taught me that ambition is not always glamorous.

Sometimes it smells like bus exhaust and cheap coffee.

Sometimes it looks like wrinkled clothes and heavy eyes.

Sometimes it means wanting something so badly that you accept inconvenience as part of the price.

Inside the Machine

Jimmy put me to work immediately.

Answer the phones.

Screen the calls.

Sort through demo CDs.

Scout raw, hungry talent.

This was before digital platforms made everything instantly accessible.

Artists mailed their dreams in plastic cases.

Hundreds of CDs stacked on desks and shelves.

Handwritten notes.

Burned discs.

Labels scribbled with Sharpie.

Each one carrying someone's belief that their music could change their life.

Sorting through those CDs became one of my favorite responsibilities.

Every disc represented hope.

A voice somewhere.

A bedroom studio somewhere.

A person believing that one song could open a door.

I understood that kind of hope intimately.

Scouting talent made me feel connected to the very thing I had once been chasing from the outside.

I was no longer just trying to get into the room.

Now I was helping decide who else got in.

That realization felt powerful.

Not in an ego-driven way.

In a purpose-driven way.

It made me pay closer attention. Not just to vocals, but to feeling. Presence. Originality. Something harder to name.

I began to trust my instincts.

Not because I thought I knew everything, but because I could feel when something moved me.

And that mattered in those rooms.

Cee

That is how I met Cee.

He was another intern at Jive.

Originally from Chicago.

Cool energy. Calm presence.

When we realized we both had ties to Columbia College Chicago, the conversation instantly flowed.

It felt like a bridge between my Chicago chapter and this new New York one.

Cee was someone I could talk to about music, about ambition, about the strange path we were both navigating.

He understood what it felt like to be near something big and still trying to figure out how to belong inside it.

One night he invited me to a gospel artist's birthday celebration at SOBs.

SOBs

SOBs was iconic.

The moment I stepped inside, I could feel the history in the room.

The walls had absorbed decades of performances.

Artists who were once unknown had stepped onto that same stage and later become legends.

The air itself felt charged.

Like the room remembered every voice that had ever passed through it.

The energy was electric.

Then he stepped on stage.

For the sake of this book, I'll call him Chuck.

Chuck wasn't just performing.

He was commanding.

His voice carried conviction. His delivery was fearless. His presence filled the entire room in a way that felt undeniable.

I had heard a lot of singers by that point.

But something about him felt different.

Authentic.

Raw.

Powerful.

He did not sound like someone trying to impress a room.

He sounded like someone who believed what he was singing.

That was the difference.

And it pulled me in immediately.

When his set ended, I walked straight up to him and handed him Jimmy's card.

"You're special," I said. "I want to set up a meeting between you and my boss."

The next day, Chuck called the office.

The meeting was set.

Jimmy listened carefully while Chuck performed.

He nodded.

Thought quietly for a moment.

Then he said something that surprised me.

"He's talented," Jimmy said, "but I already got someone like him on the roster."

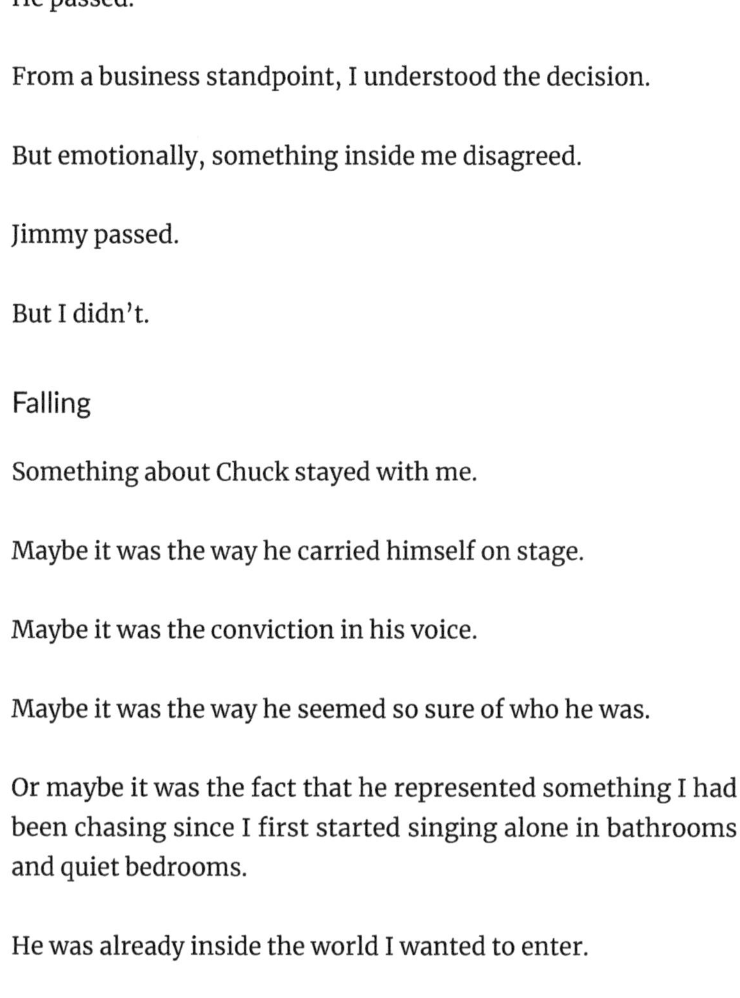

He passed.

From a business standpoint, I understood the decision.

But emotionally, something inside me disagreed.

Jimmy passed.

But I didn't.

Falling

Something about Chuck stayed with me.

Maybe it was the way he carried himself on stage.

Maybe it was the conviction in his voice.

Maybe it was the way he seemed so sure of who he was.

Or maybe it was the fact that he represented something I had been chasing since I first started singing alone in bathrooms and quiet bedrooms.

He was already inside the world I wanted to enter.

Somewhere between belief and admiration, something shifted.

What began as professional interest slowly became emotional attachment.

He was older.

Twenty-three, maybe twenty-four.

Confident.

Edgy.

Comfortable in rooms that still made my heart race.

I was nineteen.

Open-hearted.

Impressionable.

Still trying to understand what love even meant.

He moved through New York like someone who belonged to it.

I was still learning how to breathe in the city without feeling overwhelmed.

For me, it felt like love.

For him, it was probably just fun.

We were together for about three years.

At the time, I believed deeply in what we had. I believed in his music. I believed in his potential. I believed that if I stood beside him long enough, somehow we would both rise together.

I poured into him the way I pour into things I believe in.

Completely.

I listened to his dreams like they mattered to me too.

I showed up.

I supported.

I admired.

And because I was young, I mistook intensity for depth.

But love, I would later learn, does not always grow in the same direction for two people.

Sometimes one person is building.

The other is just passing through.

Back then, though, I didn't know the difference.

I just knew that I felt alive in a way I never had before.

The music industry was no longer something I observed from the outside. I was stepping deeper into it every day.

Late nights in studios.

Long conversations about songs and producers.

Artists chasing deals.

Managers chasing momentum.

Everyone chasing the same thing.

Visibility.

Success.

Validation.

New York itself felt like a character in my life during those years.

Loud.

Fast.

Unapologetic.

The subway rumbling beneath the streets.

Taxi horns echoing through intersections.

Crowded sidewalks filled with people who all seemed to be heading somewhere important.

And somehow, I had found my way into the middle of it.

I was no longer the quiet girl tucked safely into the background.

But I still had not fully learned the difference between being seen and being chosen.

Looking back now, I realize something important.

That season was about more than Chuck.

It was about identity.

I was still trying to figure out who I was.

The shy church girl.

The student who flew across the country alone.

The intern sitting quietly in industry offices.

The young woman falling in love for the first time.

All of those versions of me were colliding at once.

And the truth is, I was still searching for my voice.

Not just musically.

Personally.

Spiritually.

Emotionally.

I did not yet know that the next chapter of my life would push me even deeper into the industry.

That New York would shape me in ways I was not prepared for.

That heartbreak, ambition, creativity, and identity would collide in ways that would eventually give birth to a version of myself the world would come to know as Etta Mae.

Back then, though, I was just a nineteen-year-old girl trying to hold onto love while chasing a dream that felt bigger than anything I had ever imagined.

I thought getting in the room was the hardest part.

I had no idea the real transformation was still ahead.

* * *

5

The Break

When I decided to move to New Jersey, I told myself it was strategic.

Closer to the city.

Closer to the industry.

Closer to the life I was chasing.

But the truth is, it was also survival.

For years I had been commuting from Hartford to New York City, riding Greyhound buses before sunrise and returning long after dark. Six hours of travel every day for only a few hours inside an office had started to wear on me.

Ambition can push your mind farther than your body is meant to go.

Eventually, exhaustion catches up.

I needed to be closer.

New Jersey felt like the bridge between where I was and where I wanted to be.

My mother and my grandmother helped me move.

My grandmother had recently suffered a stroke and could no longer walk. Watching her body slow down like that was painful. The woman I had always known as strong, steady, and grounded suddenly had to rely on others for the most basic things.

But when it was time for me to pack my bags and head toward New Jersey, she insisted on coming.

She rode in the car with my mother and me.

She could not carry boxes.

She could not climb stairs.

But she came.

That meant everything.

There is something powerful about knowing the women before you are willing to push through their own pain just to see you step forward.

I remember looking at her in the back seat during the drive and realizing something I was too young to fully articulate at the time.

Legacy is not always loud.

Sometimes it is quiet support.

Sometimes it is presence.

Sometimes it is simply showing up when your body is tired but your love is stronger.

That ride to New Jersey felt like a passing of strength.

The studio apartment in Newport Pavonia was small.

Three girls sharing one tight space.

Suitcases tucked under beds.

Clothes stacked in corners.

Privacy was almost nonexistent.

But the view was breathtaking.

At sunset, the Manhattan skyline leaned against the Hudson River like it belonged there. The buildings glowed orange and gold while the water reflected their light like a mirror.

It felt cinematic.

The PATH train station was only five stops from New York City.

For the first time in my life, I felt close enough to the dream to touch it.

No more six-hour bus rides.

No more waiting in cold Greyhound terminals before sunrise.

Just a short train ride and I was in Manhattan.

The move felt like progress.

Like I was finally positioning myself where opportunities could find me.

What I didn't know was that proximity to the dream does not always mean stability inside it.

Sometimes it just means the lessons come faster.

By then, I was still tangled up with Chuck.

Three years deep.

No clarity.

No label.

No promise.

But I loved him.

Or at least I believed I did.

I had done everything for him.

I strategized marketing ideas.

Connected him to rooms.

Showed up front row at performances.

Promoted him like he was already a star.

I was his unofficial manager.

His unpaid publicist.

His number one fan.

And his hidden lover.

I convinced myself that loyalty would eventually turn into commitment.

That if I stayed long enough, worked hard enough, believed in him strongly enough, one day he would see me the way I saw him.

But love built on hope instead of reality can only survive for so long.

What I did not understand then was how easy it is to confuse devotion with destiny. When you are young and emotionally invested, you start calling your endurance love. You tell yourself that your willingness to sacrifice is proof of something meaningful. You begin to believe that if you support someone hard enough, they will eventually feel obligated to choose you.

But obligation is not love.

And being needed is not the same as being cherished.

Around that same time, my internship had ended and I landed a marketing job working under Camille Evans, a respected executive in the industry.

Camille was sharp.

Focused.

Efficient.

She moved through rooms like someone who understood exactly who she was and what she wanted.

From her, I learned things no classroom could have taught me.

How to speak with precision.

How to command attention without raising my voice.

How to hustle strategically instead of emotionally.

She carried herself with authority that didn't require explanation.

Watching her taught me something important.

Confidence is quiet when it is real.

Camille was bold.

In control.

The kind of woman I admired deeply.

And working with her gave me a glimpse of the kind of professional woman I could become.

She showed me that power did not have to be loud to be undeniable. There was no frantic energy around her. No need to impress. She simply understood her value and moved accordingly. Being around her made me realize how much of my own energy was still tied to uncertainty. I was still searching for my footing while she seemed firmly planted in hers.

But while I was growing professionally, my emotional life was quietly unraveling.

One afternoon, Ken, another intern I had met at Jive, mentioned something casually that would change everything.

Ken was also friends with Chuck.

We were talking the way people do in offices, casually exchanging updates about music, artists, and life.

Then he said something that made the air around me feel heavy.

"Did you hear Chuck's getting married?"

I froze.

For a moment I thought I had misheard him.

"What?" I asked.

"He's getting married in December."

It was October.

Just weeks earlier, I had seen Chuck.

He was still calling me.

Still spending time with me.

Still acting like we had something real.

My stomach dropped.

My hands started shaking.

I stepped away and texted him immediately.

"You're getting married? I'm never talking to you again."

A few seconds passed.

Then my phone buzzed.

"I'd be okay never talking to you again."

That sentence shattered me.

Three years.

My time.

My energy.

My ideas.

My loyalty.

My body.

My heart.

And that was it.

A single sentence.

No apology.

No explanation.

Just dismissal.

In that moment, I felt humiliated.

Disposable.

Like I had imagined something that had only ever existed in my own head.

What hurt most was not just that he was leaving.

It was how easily he did it.

How casually he reduced what felt so significant to me into something that apparently meant nothing to him. I had built entire emotional worlds around the idea of us, while he moved through it like it had all been temporary.

That kind of heartbreak does not just wound your heart.

It wounds your self-perception.

Not long after that, Chuck joined a group.

And they were huge.

Their songs were everywhere.

Taxi cabs.

Radio stations.

Shopping malls.

Even playing faintly in the waiting room at the welfare office.

I could not escape him.

Everywhere I turned, his voice followed.

While his star was rising, I felt like I was shrinking.

Success looked different when it belonged to someone who had hurt you. It was no longer just a career milestone. It became a mirror. A reminder. A soundtrack to your own disappointment. Every time I heard his voice, it was as if the city itself was reminding me that he had moved forward while I was still trying to understand what had happened.

By then, I had moved again.

This time into an overcrowded apartment in Bedford Stuyvesant, Brooklyn.

Five bedrooms.

Five strangers.

A Craigslist arrangement that was more about survival than

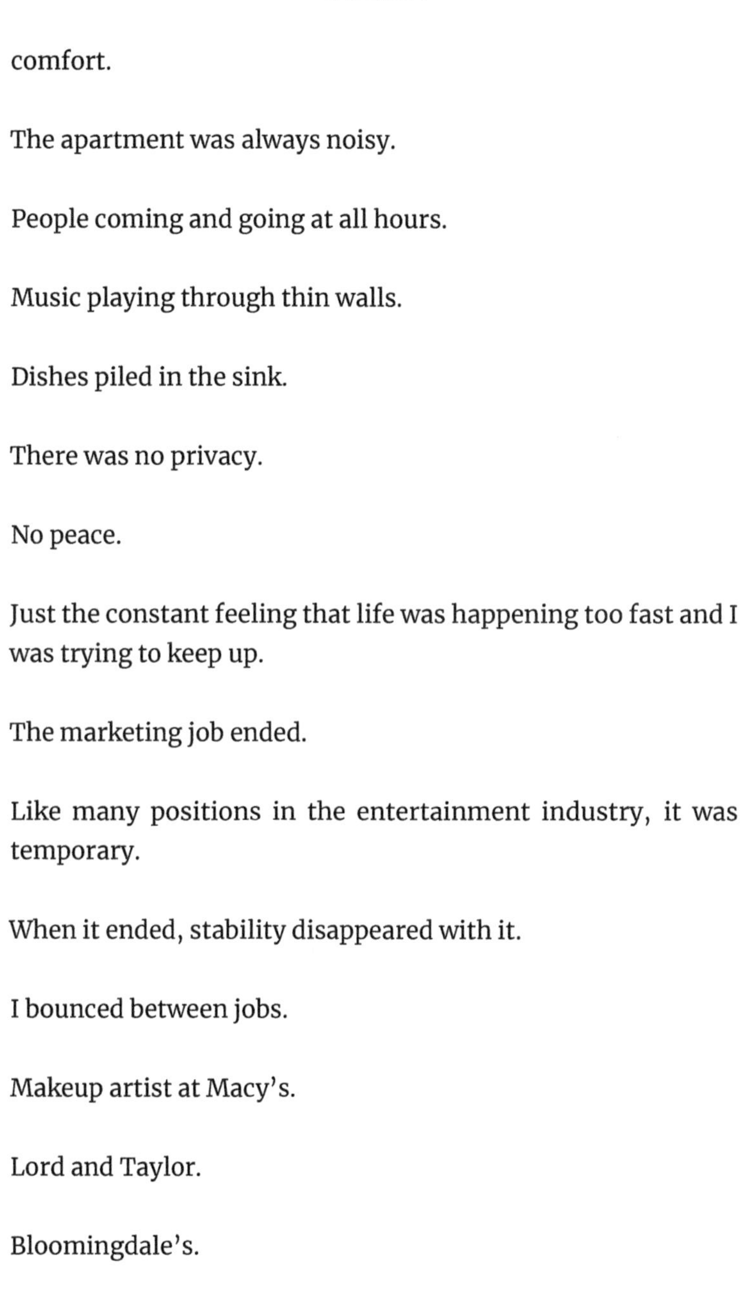

comfort.

The apartment was always noisy.

People coming and going at all hours.

Music playing through thin walls.

Dishes piled in the sink.

There was no privacy.

No peace.

Just the constant feeling that life was happening too fast and I was trying to keep up.

The marketing job ended.

Like many positions in the entertainment industry, it was temporary.

When it ended, stability disappeared with it.

I bounced between jobs.

Makeup artist at Macy's.

Lord and Taylor.

Bloomingdale's.

Temp receptionist positions in office buildings where I answered phones and pretended to feel secure.

Every day I showed up polished and professional, even when my internal world felt uncertain.

Sometimes I would sit behind the front desk watching executives walk past in expensive suits and wonder how their lives seemed so stable while mine felt like it was constantly shifting beneath my feet.

I tried to go back to school.

I enrolled determined to finish what I had started.

But without financial support, without consistent housing, balancing work and classes became impossible.

Eventually, I had to drop out again.

No degree.

No steady career.

No relationship.

No clear direction.

Just a suitcase full of dreams and a broken heart.

At the time, I thought I was failing.

Now I understand something different.

I was being formed.

The fire was not meant to destroy me.

It was refining me.

Stripping away illusions.

Teaching me boundaries.

Exposing where I had confused love with sacrifice.

I had believed proximity to greatness would make me great.

I had believed loyalty would secure love.

I had believed being useful meant being valued.

But life was teaching me a harder lesson.

Sometimes the people you pour into will still walk away.

Sometimes the rooms you fight to enter will not give you the validation you expected.

And sometimes the only person left to believe in you is you.

That season hurt deeply.

But it forced me to sit with myself.

And in that quiet, something small but powerful began to grow.

Not bitterness.

Not revenge.

Self-respect.

For the first time, I began learning how to choose myself.

Even when no one else did.

And the women who drove me to New Jersey, my mother and my grandmother, had already modeled something I did not fully understand at the time.

Strength does not always look glamorous.

Sometimes it looks like showing up anyway.

Sometimes it looks like pushing through pain just to support someone else's dream.

Sometimes it looks like quiet endurance.

That season was the soil.

And I was being planted.

* * *

6

Etta Mae Emerges

After Jive.

After Chuck.

After watching someone I once believed in become famous.

I was waiting tables at Dallas BBQ.

The irony of it all was not lost on me.

At nineteen, I had sat inside executive offices at a record label. I had sorted through demo CDs from artists across the country. I had helped discover an artist who would eventually rise in the industry.

I had been inside rooms people spent years trying to enter.

And now I was carrying trays of frozen margaritas and wiping down sticky tables.

It was humbling.

Not the pretty kind of humility that people talk about when they are already successful. The kind that confronts your ego head-on.

The kind that forces you to sit with yourself.

I ended up serving for six years.

The first three were at a smaller location, and if I am honest, I hated it.

Not because of the job.

Because of who I was.

I was operating from ego.

I carried myself like I was better than being there. Like this was temporary. Like destiny had simply placed me in the wrong room and I was waiting for someone to notice the mistake.

Energy is loud.

And mine said, *I don't belong here.*

I wasn't making the money I could have been making because my attitude showed. Some of my coworkers didn't like me. Or maybe I didn't like them.

There was tension.

Competition.

And a coldness in me that I had not yet learned how to soften.

I had gone from sitting in industry meetings to asking customers if they wanted extra sauce.

That shift bruised my pride.

Every time someone snapped their fingers for another drink or complained about their order, something in me resisted.

This isn't who I'm supposed to be.

But quietly, something else was happening beneath the surface.

Something I could not see yet.

I was being stripped down.

And sometimes that is the only way real transformation begins.

Around that time, I started smoking weed to take the edge off.

It didn't fix anything.

But it gave me a little peace, even if only for a moment.

After long shifts of smiling through frustration and carrying heavy trays across crowded rooms, that small moment of escape felt like relief.

Still, the high wore off.

And the emptiness remained.

I knew something was missing.

I needed something that would give me control again.

Not numbness.

Direction.

One night, desperate for a new habit that didn't make me feel like I was disappearing, I opened my laptop and started scrolling through Groupon.

I found a one-month gym membership at the Sheraton Hotel on 7th Avenue in Manhattan.

Thirty dollars.

I bought it immediately.

At the time, I didn't realize that decision would quietly change the course of my life.

That gym became my sanctuary.

Every day after work, I would take the train into Manhattan.

I would get off near Times Square, step onto the busy sidewalks filled with tourists and flashing lights, and walk toward the hotel.

Sometimes I would light up before going in, music blasting in my headphones as I walked through the city.

The chaos of New York would blur around me.

Taxi horns.

Crowds moving in every direction.

Street vendors calling out.

But the music in my ears created a private world.

Inside the gym, everything slowed down.

The mirrors.

The weights.

The rhythmic hum of treadmills.

The quiet concentration of people pushing their bodies past exhaustion.

It felt peaceful in a strange way.

There was a man who worked there who was always kind to me.

He never made me feel judged.

He didn't ask questions about why I was there every day or what I was going through.

He just greeted me with the same warm smile.

That meant more than he probably realized.

I started going every single day.

Not because someone told me to.

Not because I had a master plan.

But because I loved how I felt walking out.

Sweaty.

Sore.

Exhausted.

But calm.

Focused.

In control.

For the first time in a long time, I felt like I was participating in my own rescue.

No one was coming to save me.

But I could still save myself.

Rep by rep.

Day by day.

Habit by habit.

The gym gave me a reason to show up for myself again.

It became the foundation of my transformation, even though I didn't know it yet.

Around that time, I got closer to Ken.

Ken was the same intern from Jive who had once told me Chuck was getting married.

But over time, our relationship grew deeper than just industry connections.

He felt like family.

You couldn't see him without seeing me.

Ken was a talented drummer and songwriter.

He had a natural rhythm that felt effortless. Music lived inside him.

He and his partner AB, a quiet but brilliant producer, worked out of a studio where different singers would come in to record.

Sometimes I would tag along.

Watching them work felt like watching architects design sound.

Every note mattered.

Every lyric was examined.

Every breath in the microphone was intentional.

Nothing was accidental.

They would replay sections over and over again until it felt right.

Perfecting the smallest details.

I soaked it all in.

The studio felt like a classroom.

But this time, the lessons were alive.

No textbooks.

No syllabi.

Just instinct, repetition, taste, and discipline.

That was when I started writing seriously.

Not just journaling.

Songs.

Melodies.

Hooks.

Verses.

Emotions that had been sitting inside me for years finally had somewhere to go.

Heartbreak turned into lyrics.

Confusion turned into melodies.

Frustration turned into rhythm.

I started understanding something powerful.

Music wasn't just something I loved.

It was something that lived inside me.

It had always lived there.

It had been waiting for me to stop running from myself long enough to hear it clearly.

At the same time, my body was changing.

Between serving tables and working out every day, I had dropped a noticeable amount of weight.

One day during that season at the first BBQ location, I finally got my braces removed.

I remember sitting in the dentist's chair when they handed me a mirror.

I stared at my reflection for a long moment.

My smile looked different.

Straighter.

Brighter.

But it wasn't just my teeth that had changed.

Something inside me had shifted too.

Confidence crept in.

Not loud.

Not flashy.

Just present.

Steady.

I no longer looked at myself and only saw what was missing.

I started seeing potential.

I started seeing shape.

Presence.

Possibility.

For so long, I had been behind the scenes supporting other people's dreams.

But now I had something to say.

One day I looked down at the tattoo on my forearm.

Etta Mae.

My grandmother's name.

A woman who carried strength quietly.

A woman who showed up for me even when her own body was weak.

That tattoo had always been meaningful to me.

But suddenly it felt like something more.

One of my friends noticed it one day and said, "Yo... that would be a dope artist name."

I paused.

Something clicked immediately.

Etta Mae.

It sounded strong.

Rooted.

Grounded.

It carried history.

Legacy.

It sounded like a woman who had survived something.

A woman who understood softness and strength at the same time.

And suddenly the idea felt obvious.

Etta Mae the artist was born.

What I didn't fully understand yet was that I needed her.

Shauna was still healing.

Still tender.

Still unsure.

Etta Mae gave me somewhere to place the confidence I was slowly growing into.

She became the version of me that could walk into a room without apologizing.

Around that same time, I met Malachi.

It was Halloween.

He came into the restaurant with a group of friends, all of them dressed in elaborate costumes.

His stood out immediately.

Creative.

Detailed.

Confident.

The entire group had a loud energy, but in the best way.

They were having fun without being obnoxious.

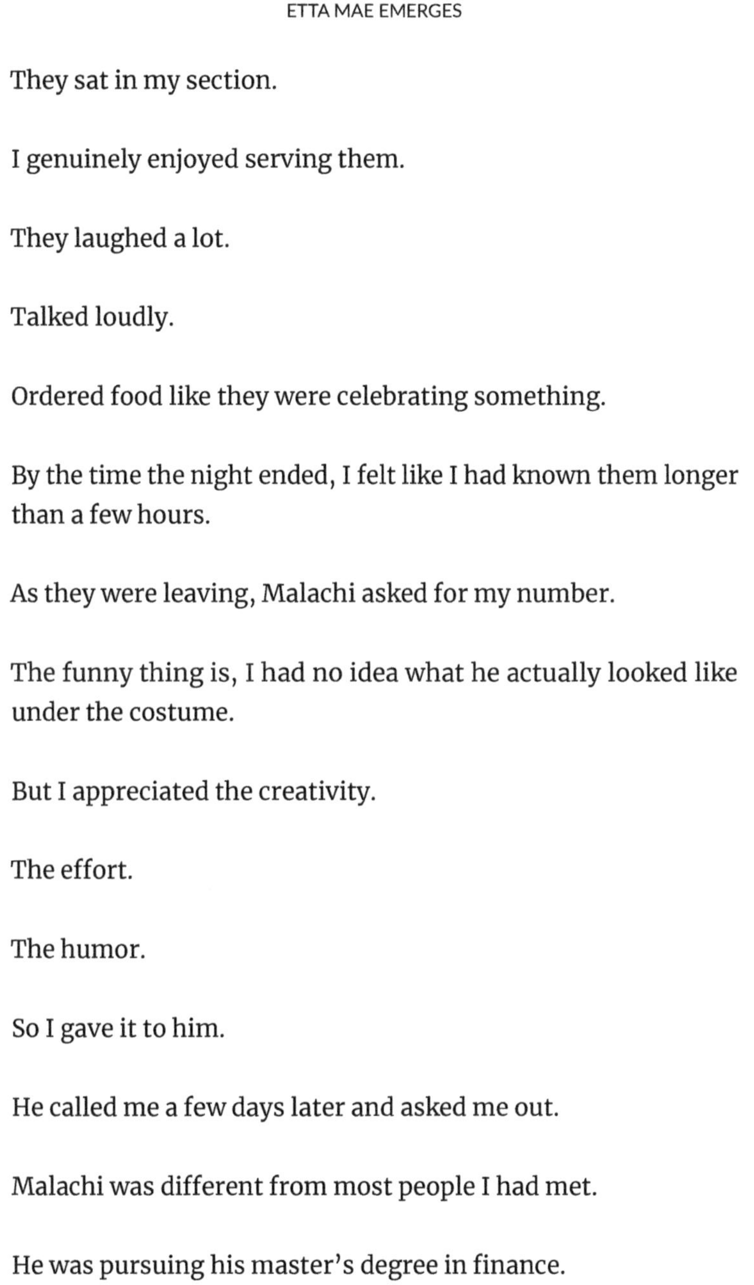

They sat in my section.

I genuinely enjoyed serving them.

They laughed a lot.

Talked loudly.

Ordered food like they were celebrating something.

By the time the night ended, I felt like I had known them longer than a few hours.

As they were leaving, Malachi asked for my number.

The funny thing is, I had no idea what he actually looked like under the costume.

But I appreciated the creativity.

The effort.

The humor.

So I gave it to him.

He called me a few days later and asked me out.

Malachi was different from most people I had met.

He was pursuing his master's degree in finance.

That intrigued me.

Structured.

Academic.

Focused.

But he also had another side.

He was a party promoter.

He knew nightlife.

He knew club owners.

He knew how to gather people and create energy inside a room.

Finance by day.

Nightlife by night.

That balance fascinated me.

We spent a lot of time together.

He would pick me up from work when my shifts ended late.

That mattered.

In a season where I often felt overlooked, his presence felt steady.

He represented another kind of possibility too.

He showed me that a person could move between worlds.

Practical and creative.

Disciplined and social.

Ambitious in more than one direction.

But if I am honest, our relationship was chaotic at times.

Not because he was reckless.

Because I had not yet mastered my emotions.

I was still healing.

Still reactive.

Still sensitive.

Still trying to prove my worth without realizing it.

Small disagreements felt bigger than they needed to be.

I had not yet learned how to regulate my feelings instead of letting them spill over.

I was still carrying unresolved pain into present moments and calling it passion.

We lasted about three years.

But we were both still becoming.

Eventually, we let each other go.

After three years at the smaller Dallas BBQ location, I transferred to a bigger one.

And something inside me shifted.

Instead of resenting the job, I decided to master it.

I studied serving like it was performance.

I watched how experienced servers worked a room.

How they spoke.

How they carried trays.

How they built rapport with customers.

I learned how to read people within seconds.

How to adjust my tone.

How to anticipate needs before they were spoken.

How to make someone celebrating feel important.

How to make someone having a bad day feel seen.

I made every customer who sat in my section feel special.

And I became very good at it.

So good that customers began coming in weekly asking to sit in my section.

That was when something clicked.

If I could build loyalty in a restaurant, I could build loyalty anywhere.

I started to understand that service was not small work.

It was relational work.

It taught me how to connect quickly, how to make people feel comfortable, how to leave an impression.

Those same skills mattered in music.

In branding.

In performance.

In life.

So I started inviting my customers to my shows.

At first it felt awkward.

"Hey, I'm performing this weekend. You should come."

Some of them did.

Then they brought friends.

Then those friends brought other people.

Slowly, I was building an audience.

Not through radio.

Not through a label.

Through relationships.

Serving tables had taught me something the music industry hadn't.

Connection.

People don't support you because of marketing.

They support you because they feel something when they meet you.

They support authenticity.

They support energy.

They support the feeling you leave behind after the interaction is over.

That lesson stayed with me.

And it would help shape everything I built later.

Confidence was no longer creeping in.

It was settling in.

I wasn't chasing rooms anymore.

I was building myself.

And that changed everything.

* * *

7

Armor and Isolation

By now, Shauna had taken a back seat to someone new.

Someone bolder.

Louder.

More provocative.

I was Etta Mae.

She was not just a stage name.

She was armor.

A permission slip to be powerful and unapologetically feminine. A version of myself that did not tremble before entering rooms. A version that did not apologize for being seen.

Shauna had spent years shrinking.

Etta Mae expanded.

With a newly sculpted body, high cheekbones sharpened by weight loss, and a confidence I had never known before, I began doing photoshoots that were daring.

Scantily clad.

Sensual.

Commanding attention.

The first time I stepped in front of a camera in lingerie, my pulse raced.

Not from shame.

From power.

The photographer adjusted the lights and studied me carefully, walking slowly around the room like an artist studying a sculpture.

"Relax your shoulders," he said.

"Look directly into the lens."

"Own it."

I thought about every time I had been overlooked.

Every time someone had spoken over me.

Every time I had felt invisible.

And I owned it.

Flash.

Flash.

Flash.

Something shifted inside me that day.

For years I had been the quiet girl standing in the background. The one supporting everyone else. The one observing the room rather than commanding it.

But in front of that camera, I felt seen.

The photographers loved me.

They told me I had presence. That I carried something magnetic. They said the camera responded to me.

They posed me in ways that made jaws drop.

Legs crossed slightly.

Hair falling across my shoulders.

Eyes locked into the lens with quiet confidence.

I did not just look sexy.

I learned how to exude it.

Word began to spread in small creative circles around New York. One photoshoot led to another. Stylists reached out wanting collaborations. Designers with small clothing lines wanted their pieces photographed on my body.

Sometimes the shoots took place in tiny Brooklyn apartments where the living room had been turned into a makeshift studio.

Other times they happened in rented loft spaces in Manhattan where sunlight poured through tall industrial windows.

Music always played.

Usually something soulful.

The photographers would move around me slowly, adjusting angles and lighting while the room buzzed with creative energy.

Click.

Click.

Click.

Each flash felt like affirmation.

For years I had been told to stay small.

Now the world was asking me to take up space.

And I did.

There was something addictive about being looked at and finally feeling in control of how I was seen. For so long, people had projected things onto me. Their expectations. Their assumptions. Their doubts. But in those photo shoots, I got to shape the image. I got to decide what strength looked like on my body. What femininity looked like in my face. What power looked like through my own eyes.

That mattered more than I could fully articulate at the time.

Back home, church circles whispered.

My grandmother's name, Etta Mae, was sacred.

She had been a First Lady.

Soft spoken.

Graceful.

Known for her quiet strength and modest dresses that fell below her knees.

To some people, what I was doing felt like blasphemy. Like I had wrapped something holy in something provocative.

But in New York, Etta Mae was adored.

The city rewarded boldness.

People in the industry started calling me The Black Marilyn Monroe.

At first, it felt intoxicating.

Iconic.

To be compared to a cultural symbol of beauty and sensuality felt like arrival.

Marilyn Monroe represented glamour and allure. Hearing that comparison made me feel like I had stepped into a legacy of women who knew how to command attention without saying a word.

But late at night, when the makeup was washed off and the cameras were gone, I would sometimes think about Marilyn.

Beautiful.

Desired.

Watched.

And lonely.

Fame and loneliness often live in the same house.

I did not want to be admired and abandoned in the same breath.

That was the strange thing about becoming Etta Mae. She made me feel powerful in public, but power does not always follow you home. There were nights when I would leave a shoot or a performance feeling electric, only to come back to silence and realize that being desired and being deeply known are not the same thing.

Music became my lifeline.

I released two EPs under the name Etta Mae: *Chuck* and *Malachi.*

Each project carried pieces of my story.

Every song held buried emotion. The heartbreaks I once tried to swallow became melodies.

The disappointments I once tried to hide became lyrics.

Pain has a way of turning into art when you refuse to let it stay silent.

I released singles in between.

Always writing.

Always recording.

Always searching for the sound that felt most honest.

And honesty, I was learning, does not always arrive softly. Sometimes it comes through a lyric that sounds prettier than the truth it came from. Sometimes it hides inside a hook. Sometimes it slips into a verse and only reveals itself to you later.

The shows started coming.

Dive bars where the floors were sticky and the speakers crackled.

Lounges where the lighting was low and intimate.

Community stages where the crowd talked loudly until you earned their attention.

Every performance was a test.

Could you hold a room?

Could you make people stop talking long enough to listen?

Some nights the audience leaned in.

Other nights they barely looked up.

Either way, I kept singing.

Because every stage was preparation for the next one.

I learned how to perform through distraction. Through noise. Through indifference. I learned that talent is only part of the equation. Presence matters too. Energy matters. Whether or not the room believes you matters. And if the room doesn't believe you at first, you have to believe yourself enough for both of you.

Around that time, something surreal happened.

I was cast as background in the Netflix series *She's Gotta Have It*, directed by Spike Lee.

Standing on that set felt like standing inside a cultural moment.

Lights.

Cameras.

Actors rehearsing scenes about love and identity in Brooklyn.

I stood just outside the frame.

Close enough to feel the creative energy moving through the room.

Watching that process reminded me that culture is built by people who refuse to stay quiet.

And I was slowly finding my place within it.

Then came one of the most terrifying performances of my life.

Opening for Fantasia.

Backstage, the energy was electric.

Stagehands moved quickly between equipment. Performers warmed up their voices in quiet corners. The bass from the crowd vibrated faintly through the floor.

I peeked through the curtain and saw the audience stretching across the venue.

Hundreds of faces.

Some excited.

Some impatient.

Some already loyal to the headliner they came to see.

In moments like that, the opening act can feel invisible.

Or disposable.

When the stage manager gave me the signal, my heart pounded so loudly I thought the microphone might pick it up.

The second I stepped on stage, the crowd booed.

Loudly.

Instantly.

The sound hit me in the chest like a physical force.

For a split second, I considered walking off.

But something inside me refused to fold.

I lifted the microphone.

And I sang.

My voice trembled at first.

Then it steadied.

I locked into the melody like it was a rope pulling me forward.

Halfway through the song, something shifted.

The boos softened.

A few cheers rose.

By the time I finished my set, the audience was clapping.

That night taught me something important about myself.

I do not fold easily.

That lesson mattered far beyond the stage. It reminded me that rejection does not have to be the end of a moment. Sometimes you have to sing through the noise long enough for people to hear you clearly. Sometimes the same room that resists you at first can be won over if you do not abandon yourself too quickly.

The stages kept getting bigger.

I performed at the United Nations.

Standing inside a building where global conversations took place felt surreal. I thought about the girl who once sat quietly in church pews, too shy to raise her voice.

And there I was.

Singing.

Then came a moment that felt almost spiritual.

I stepped onto the stage at SOBs.

Years earlier I had stood inside that same venue watching someone else perform.

That night, I was no longer the girl observing from the crowd.

I was center stage.

There was something sacred about that full-circle moment. It reminded me that life has a way of bringing you back to certain places so you can see how much you have changed. What had once felt unattainable was now happening under my own feet.

But success has a way of magnifying absence.

During that season, I moved into my own apartment for the first time.

No roommates.

No shared refrigerator.

No overlapping lives.

Just me.

A rent-stabilized studio in East New York.

Seven hundred dollars a month.

When I first unlocked the door, the space echoed.

I stood in the middle of the room listening to the silence.

I painted the accent wall red.

Bold.

Loud.

Impossible to ignore.

I bought a red leather couch and hung artwork that made the room feel alive.

It was not glamorous.

But it was mine.

At night, when the city quieted and the train hummed in the distance, the silence felt heavier.

Sometimes I would come home from performances still wearing stage makeup and sit on that red couch staring at the quiet room.

No applause.

No music.

Just the low hum of the refrigerator and distant trains.

Those were the moments when Shauna returned.

Etta Mae thrived in front of crowds.

Shauna lived in the quiet spaces between them.

I missed my siblings.

By then I had not spoken to them in years.

I did not have their numbers.

I did not even know where they lived.

The disowning had not happened overnight.

It was the consequence of choosing truth over silence.

Years earlier I had testified in court to protect my siblings' right to an education.

Responsibility comes with a price.

After that, my mother cut me off completely.

No calls.

No updates.

No siblings.

Just silence.

So while people in New York were calling me The Black Marilyn Monroe, I was also a daughter without a family.

While I was stepping onto stages, I was grieving quietly in a red apartment.

That duality shaped me more than the spotlight ever could.

It is one thing to be praised in public.

It is another thing entirely to sit alone with your own ache when the night ends.

That season taught me that applause cannot replace intimacy. Success cannot always soften loneliness. And the versions of ourselves we build to survive can sometimes keep other people out while they protect us.

Around that time, I met a well-known rapper through a former coworker.

For the sake of this book, I will call him Rico.

Rico had presence.

Street edge.

Confidence that felt almost dangerous.

The kind of man who filled a room without raising his voice.

I was drawn in.

One night I returned to the studio alone to play him my music.

He listened.

Nodded.

Said I had something.

That was enough to pull me deeper into his orbit.

I kept returning.

Eventually I had the door code.

We were intimate once.

Looking back now, I can see my naivety clearly.

He lived in a world built on image and dominance.

I lived in melody and vulnerability.

But at the time, I told myself proximity meant progress.

He is popular.

He is on.

He can help me.

Then came the reality show offer.

A major production wanted him for the next season.

And he wanted me to be part of his storyline.

The role?

The side chick.

He said it casually.

Strategically.

Like it was opportunity.

In that moment, everything inside me sharpened.

I thought about the courtroom where I had once stood at fourteen telling the truth.

I thought about the stages where I had been booed but kept singing.

I thought about the years it took to build myself.

I had not come this far to reduce myself to someone else's storyline.

Fame whispers seductive lies.

It tells you dignity can wait.

But I knew the cost.

So I walked away.

Quietly.

Decisively.

Do I regret stepping into those studio spaces?

Yes.

Did I learn from them?

Absolutely.

That season taught me something I still carry today.

Access is not alignment.

Proximity to power is not power.

And dignity is worth more than visibility.

In that red apartment in East New York, with a red wall and a red couch, I began to understand something deeper.

Etta Mae was never meant to replace Shauna.

She was meant to protect her.

But protection and isolation are not the same thing.

Eventually, I would have to learn how to live without armor.

And that lesson was waiting just ahead.

* * *

8

Wilderness

When I learned what role Rico wanted me to play in his reality show storyline, everything inside me screamed no.

The side chick.

That was never going to be my legacy.

I had worked too hard to reclaim myself. I was not about to sell my self-worth for screen time, no matter how tempting the exposure might have been.

So I quietly began my exit plan.

I told Rico I was moving to Los Angeles.

He was cold.

There were no questions in his voice. No curiosity about why I had made that decision. No attempt to convince me to stay.

He barely reacted at all.

And I could feel exactly why.

His plan to have the best storyline reality television had ever seen was falling apart. He knew without me there would be no tension. No emotional triangle for producers to stretch across episodes. No drama for the cameras to follow.

He was not losing a woman.

He was losing a plot.

The last time I went to the studio before leaving, she was there too.

The girl.

The one who was supposed to play the role of the "main" woman in this carefully designed reality television story.

As soon as I walked in, she rolled her eyes at me like I was a nuisance.

It was around Christmas time.

Despite everything, I had brought two small gifts for Rico's children.

I didn't come with attitude.

I didn't come with drama.

I came with kindness.

I handed him the gifts.

He didn't even say thank you.

That moment sealed everything for me.

I realized something I probably should have understood much earlier.

I was never valued.

I was leveraged.

A storyline.

A prop.

A spark for drama.

And I was done.

The biggest reason I wanted to leave was opportunity.

I wanted to see what doors might open in Hollywood. Film. Television. Bigger creative rooms. Different energy.

New York had shaped me.

But I felt a ceiling there.

And I wanted expansion.

I called my aunt in California.

She had a calming voice, the kind that lowers your blood pressure just by hearing it. Soft spoken. Gentle.

I told her I was ready to relocate to Los Angeles to seriously pursue music.

She didn't hesitate.

"Come on out," she said.

That was all I needed.

At the time, my credit was flawless.

I walked into a dealership in Brooklyn and walked out with a Toyota RAV4.

No down payment.

Just keys and a dream.

I packed my entire life into that car.

Clothes.

Shoes.

Hard drives filled with songs.

Stage outfits.

Notebooks full of lyrics.

Makeup.

Headshots.

Pieces of the woman I was becoming and remnants of the girl I used to be.

Before leaving New York, I cut all my hair off.

New energy.

New beginning.

Sometimes you have to shed the old version of yourself physically before you can step into the next chapter emotionally.

That haircut felt symbolic. I looked in the mirror and saw less softness, less hiding. There was something bold about it. Something stripped down and honest. I had spent so many years becoming different versions of myself depending on the room I was in. This time, I wanted the road to introduce me to someone truer.

The drive to California took three days.

Three long days on highways that stretched endlessly across the country.

I created a playlist of my own music and let it play on repeat as I crossed state lines.

There is something surreal about listening to your own voice while watching entire landscapes pass by your windshield.

At gas stations I would stretch my legs and look around at strangers passing through their own journeys.

Everyone was headed somewhere.

Truck drivers.

Families.

Couples arguing quietly beside their cars.

People buying coffee at strange hours of the night.

And there I was, carrying everything I owned in the back of an SUV, driving toward a future I could not see clearly but desperately wanted to believe in.

Somewhere in Tennessee I got a speeding ticket that made my stomach drop.

Unexpected expenses were the last thing I needed.

But there was no turning back now.

I paid it and kept driving.

The further west I drove, the more the air began to feel different.

By the time I reached California, I felt something inside me loosen.

This was supposed to be my new beginning.

I didn't have a job lined up.

But I had always been good at figuring things out.

I registered my car.

Got a California ID.

And started driving for Lyft.

It was honest money.

I met people.

Learned the city.

Heard stories.

I networked from the driver's seat.

Some passengers were tourists.

Some were creatives chasing dreams similar to mine.

Some were just people trying to get home after long days.

Every ride felt like a small window into someone else's life.

For a moment, it felt like things were stabilizing.

I even tried going back to school.

But tension inside my aunt's home slowly began to grow.

At first it was subtle.

Small comments.

Side glances.

Questions that felt less like curiosity and more like judgment.

My aunt and cousins did not seem to respect the version of pursuing music that included working a regular job or enrolling in classes.

They wanted the fantasy version of the dream.

Studio sessions.

Networking events.

Social media posts.

Full-time chasing.

But I saw a different reality.

Bills had to be paid.

Dreams do not always pay rent.

I was no longer interested in starving for the appearance of passion. I had already lived through enough instability to know that ambition without structure can become self-destruction. Wanting something badly is not the same as building wisely toward it.

The argument that ended everything started over something small.

Detergent.

Words escalated.

Energy shifted.

Voices got louder.

And suddenly I was being told to leave.

Just like that.

No plan.

No backup.

Just gone.

I called another cousin who lived about twenty minutes away.

She had a room for rent.

Seven hundred dollars a month.

I moved in.

But I was homesick.

I missed New York.

The rhythm of the trains.

The familiar streets.

The chaotic energy that once fueled my ambition.

And if I was honest with myself, I missed Rico too.

Not because he was good for me.

But because familiarity can feel like comfort, even when it's poison.

To reconnect with something that felt familiar, I flew back to New York a few times.

Quick visits.

Just enough to refill my soul.

But those trips drained my money.

When rent came due, I was short.

One hundred and fifty dollars.

That was it.

Just one hundred and fifty dollars.

I asked my cousin for one day.

Just one.

She refused.

"Get out. Right now."

Just like that, I was homeless.

There is something surreal about realizing your life has changed in a single sentence. One moment you are asking for a little grace. The next, you are calculating where you can park without being noticed. Pride does not leave all at once. It leaves in layers.

I moved most of my belongings into a storage unit.

Thirty dollars a month.

It became my closet.

Every few days I would stop there to grab clothes or shoes before going about my day.

That storage unit held everything I owned.

A silent reminder of how small my life had suddenly become.

With nowhere else to go, I started sleeping in my car.

That season of my life is blurry.

Cold.

Humbling.

I parked in grocery store parking lots.

Rest stops.

Random residential streets where I hoped no one would notice me.

I kept wipes in the glove compartment.

Snacks in the trunk.

Water bottles.

My dreams somewhere in the rearview mirror.

At night, I would recline the seat as far back as I could and try to rest. Some nights were quiet. Other nights every sound felt threatening. Headlights passing. A car door slamming nearby. Someone walking too close. I learned how exposed a person can feel when they have nowhere to fully close the world out.

I tried to keep going to school, but survival took over.

I dropped out again.

The dream paused.

Reality took center stage.

I drove Lyft.

Picked up strangers.

Smiled.

Made conversation.

Dropped them off at homes I wished I had.

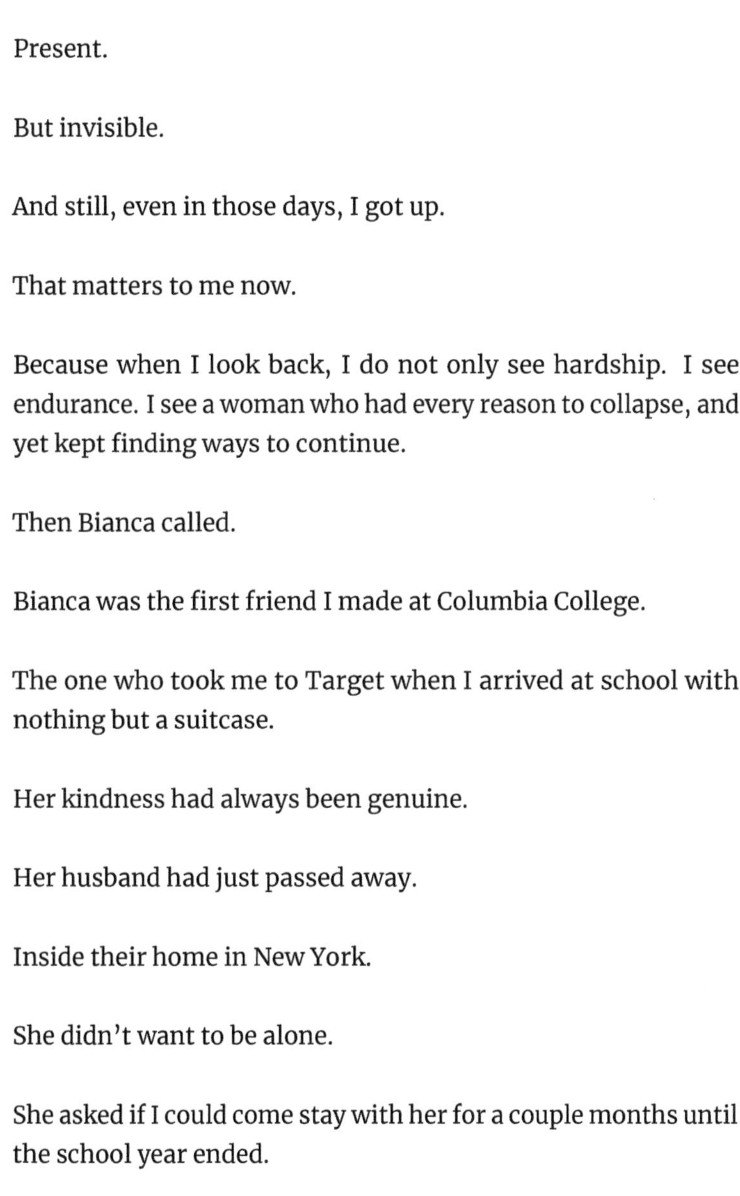

Some days I felt like a ghost in a city full of stars.

Present.

But invisible.

And still, even in those days, I got up.

That matters to me now.

Because when I look back, I do not only see hardship. I see endurance. I see a woman who had every reason to collapse, and yet kept finding ways to continue.

Then Bianca called.

Bianca was the first friend I made at Columbia College.

The one who took me to Target when I arrived at school with nothing but a suitcase.

Her kindness had always been genuine.

Her husband had just passed away.

Inside their home in New York.

She didn't want to be alone.

She asked if I could come stay with her for a couple months until the school year ended.

I said yes immediately.

I drove back across the country.

Back to New York.

Back to the place that held so many versions of me.

We grieved together.

Her grief was immediate.

Heavy.

The kind that fills the room even when no one is speaking.

Mine was layered.

I was grieving instability.

Lost direction.

The life I thought I would be living by now.

I applied at IHOP and started working there.

From industry rooms to pancake refills.

From stage lights to syrup bottles.

It stung more than I wanted to admit.

I had once believed my life would move upward in a straight line.

Instead it kept looping back to survival.

There is a particular kind of pain in feeling like you have already seen the version of life you wanted, only to find yourself standing somewhere that feels like the opposite of it. Every plate I carried at IHOP reminded me that nothing in my journey had unfolded the way I thought it would. But it also kept me fed. Sometimes humility looks like accepting what keeps you alive.

The RAV4 was barely hanging on during that time.

I had fallen behind on payments.

One morning I woke up and it was gone.

Repossessed.

No warning.

No conversation.

Just absence.

I called and learned I had three days to come up with one thousand dollars plus towing fees.

I didn't have it.

And I had no one to ask.

Something inside me broke that day.

I started taking the bus to work.

Sometimes Bianca would pick me up after my shifts.

Standing at the bus stop in my uniform felt like watching my pride bleed slowly.

In that moment, I wanted nothing to do with music.

The industry felt like a bad relationship I kept crawling back to.

I needed space.

Clarity.

Time to remember who I was without the pressure of success.

When summer came, Bianca moved to Maryland.

And I returned to California.

Still restless.

Still searching.

This time I had no car.

But I discovered Lyft's Express Drive program.

They rented vehicles to drivers for weekly payments.

I signed up immediately.

Wheels again.

A sliver of independence.

I rotated between Airbnb rentals.

Living out of bags.

Living lightly because I had no other choice.

The strange thing about that season was how normal I looked on the outside.

Even while struggling, I was still getting invited to A-list Hollywood parties.

Many people I had met in the New York music scene were now living in Los Angeles.

They invited me out.

They had no idea what my reality looked like.

And I hid it well.

Years of working as a makeup artist taught me presentation.

Style.

Confidence.

No one could see the instability behind it.

But I could feel it.

Certain rooms carried a strange energy.

A darkness.

Not something visible.

Something spiritual.

The atmosphere felt thick with secrets.

People wearing masks and calling it networking.

At those parties, everyone seemed polished, lit just right, performing some version of certainty. But underneath it all I could feel how hollow some of it was. How desperate. How transactional. It made me question what I was really trying to reach for.

One night, I felt unsafe.

Emotionally.

Spiritually.

Maybe even physically.

I couldn't sleep.

The next morning, I got in my Lyft rental and drove north toward San Francisco.

A friend from college lived there, but he was out of the country.

So I booked an Airbnb nearby and crashed.

The host messaged me the next day.

"Are you coming back?"

Most Airbnb hosts don't check in like that after checkout.

But something about his message felt different.

Almost intuitive.

Like he sensed I needed somewhere safe.

He offered me a private room in his house for thirty dollars a night.

I said yes.

I turned the car around.

Picked up my belongings from storage in Los Angeles.

And moved in.

I stayed there for months.

Driving Lyft.

Surviving.

Trying to rebuild something inside myself.

Then came the ride that changed everything.

I was parked outside a grocery store when I received a ride request.

The woman called immediately.

"I'm actually at the Mexican restaurant around the corner," she said.

I drove around and picked her up.

Her name was Diane.

She had a calm spirit that immediately put me at ease.

During the short drive I asked what she did.

"I'm a piano teacher," she said.

Something inside me lit up.

"I'm a singer-songwriter," I replied.

The ride lasted maybe five minutes.

But before she got out, she invited me inside to see her studio.

A grand piano sat in the middle of her living room like a throne.

I told her I couldn't afford lessons.

But I gave her my number anyway.

"If you ever need a ride," I said, "I got you."

She called the next day.

"Want to have lunch?" she asked.

We met.

We talked.

And then she offered me something that felt like divine timing.

"Be my driver," she said. "Take me on errands. In return, I'll give you free piano lessons."

I said yes immediately.

And just like that, life shifted.

That five-minute Lyft ride became the pivot my soul needed.

Diane didn't just teach me piano.

She reminded me of music's magic.

She reminded me who I was underneath the pain, the alter egos, the failures, and the labels.

She helped me return to music.

Not for fame.

Not for validation.

But for me.

And for the first time in a long time, I wasn't chasing anything.

I was returning.

* * *

9

Unexpected Doors

Sometimes the people who change your life the most begin as complete strangers.

Diane was one of those people.

I met her through Lyft.

At the time, I was living in Northern California, doing my best to survive. I was driving Lyft every day just to keep money coming in. My life felt fragile. Temporary. I had been bouncing from city to city, from one unstable situation to another. My confidence had been shaken by years of uncertainty. I was exhausted in a way that sleep could not fix.

I had spent so much time in survival mode that I barely knew how to imagine a future anymore. My days were built around making it through. Where would I sleep? How much money could I make today? How long could I keep stretching what little I had? Even when I smiled, even when I looked put together, there was a constant instability underneath it all.

One afternoon I was sitting in a grocery store parking lot waiting for my next ride request when a ping came through. A woman called almost immediately after the ride was accepted.

"I'm actually at the Mexican restaurant around the corner," she said, sounding slightly annoyed.

I drove around the corner and found her standing outside the restaurant.

She got into the car, and immediately her presence felt calm. She was not overly talkative. Not guarded either. Just grounded. There was something settled about her spirit, something that made me feel like I could exhale a little.

Her name was Diane.

We started talking during the ride, and I asked her what she did for work.

"I'm a piano teacher," she said.

Something inside me lit up instantly.

"I'm a singer-songwriter," I told her.

The ride was short, barely five minutes, but before she stepped out, she said something unexpected.

"Do you want to come inside and see my studio?"

I hesitated for a moment, but curiosity won.

Inside her home sat a beautiful grand piano. It looked almost regal in the room, like it had a presence of its own. I walked around it slowly the way someone might walk around a sculpture in a museum, trying not to touch it too quickly, trying to take in the fullness of what I was seeing.

I told her I wished I could take lessons, but I could not afford them.

Before I left, I gave her my number and told her that if she ever needed a ride, I would gladly come pick her up.

The next day she called.

"Would you like to have lunch?" she asked.

That lunch turned into a conversation that would shift my life.

After we finished eating, she made me an offer.

"Be my driver," she said. "Take me on errands. In return, I will give you piano lessons."

I said yes without hesitation.

And just like that, our routine began.

Every morning at exactly 10:30 a.m., I would pull into her driveway.

She would come out with her purse tucked under her arm, always composed, always ready for the day. Our routine was simple but meaningful. We ran errands together. Sometimes the bank. Sometimes the grocery store. Sometimes the post office or pharmacy.

Nothing glamorous.

Just everyday life.

But those quiet errands became the most stabilizing part of my week.

There is something sacred about consistency when your life has been chaos for so long. Knowing that every morning I would see Diane, that we would move through the day together, that I had somewhere to be and someone expecting me, gave my life a rhythm it had been missing.

No matter what we did that morning, we always ended with lunch.

After lunch, we returned to her home, and that is when the real work began.

I would sit down at the grand piano.

Diane did not treat me like someone casually dabbling in music. She taught me with the seriousness of someone preparing a real musician. She expected me to pay attention. She expected me to improve. She expected me to respect the craft.

She taught me music theory.

She taught me how to read notes properly instead of relying solely on my ear.

She taught me how chords were built, why certain progressions create tension, and how harmony works.

She taught me how to write music.

She challenged me.

She corrected me.

She pushed me.

And I loved every minute of it.

For the first time in a long time, music did not feel like performance. It did not feel like branding. It did not feel like survival. It felt pure again. It felt like returning to something sacred.

This rhythm continued for nearly a year.

But Diane gave me much more than music.

She entered my life at one of the darkest seasons I had ever experienced.

During that time, I would wake up drenched in cold sweats. My body was constantly tense. I had spent so many months living in survival mode that my nervous system no longer knew how to relax.

I had no real safety net.

No family nearby.

No consistent direction.

Just survival.

I was at rock bottom.

And somehow this woman, who had met me through a five-minute Lyft ride, took me under her wing.

Even now, when I think about it, I am moved by the simplicity of that kindness. She did not know my whole story. She did not know all the places I had been or all the ways I had fallen. She just recognized something in me worth investing in.

She told me stories about her life in the music industry. Artists she had encountered. The difference between talent and discipline. The way some people waste their gifts because they never build the habits needed to sustain them.

She did not glamorize the industry.

She humanized it.

That helped me more than she probably realized.

By then, I had already seen enough of the music world to know that talent alone was not enough. I had seen people with amazing gifts sabotage themselves. I had seen how image could open doors, but character determined whether you could stay in the room. Diane helped me understand that musicianship was about more than expression. It was about study. Practice. Humility. Repetition.

Eventually Diane invited me to Thanksgiving dinner with her family.

That invitation meant more to me than words could express.

I had been disconnected from my own family for years. Holidays had become quiet, sometimes lonely reminders of what I had lost. I was used to watching other people gather while I found ways to make myself feel less alone.

But that Thanksgiving I sat at a table surrounded by warmth.

I listened to family stories.

Laughter moved through the room.

Plates were passed.

Voices overlapped.

And for a moment, I felt like I belonged somewhere again.

Diane also taught me about something I had never thought about before.

Bartering.

The idea that value can be exchanged in many ways, not just through money.

She believed deeply in that philosophy. Our entire relationship was built on it. I drove her where she needed to go. In return, she invested in my musical growth.

That exchange reshaped how I thought about work, value, and relationships.

It reminded me that I still had something to offer, even in a season when I felt stripped down by life.

Another passion Diane had was politics.

She followed political news closely and spoke about government and policy in ways that fascinated me. At first, I struggled to keep up with her conversations. She referenced historical events, Supreme Court decisions, and philosophical ideas with an ease I admired.

If I wanted to truly engage with her conversations, I realized I needed to learn more.

So I enrolled at Foothill College in Palo Alto, California.

I decided to major in political science.

At first, it felt like an unusual choice. I had always seen myself primarily as an artist. But the more classes I took, the more captivated I became.

American history suddenly felt alive.

Not the simplified version we hear growing up, but the complicated reality behind it. The contradictions. The ideals. The hypocrisy. The courage. The systems that shaped the country and the people trapped within those systems.

I became fascinated with the philosophical ideas behind government.

John Locke.

Thomas Hobbes.

The social contract.

The tension between liberty and order.

The question of who gets power, how they get it, and who gets left out.

For someone who had felt powerless during many parts of my childhood, learning about power structures felt empowering.

Politics also became impossible to ignore.

This was during the Trump presidency, and politics seemed

to dominate every news cycle. It was on television constantly. Social media discussions. Heated debates everywhere.

Politics almost felt like entertainment.

But in the classroom it became something deeper.

It became analysis.

It became history, power, language, law, consequence.

And once I began to understand it, I loved it.

This was also during the height of COVID.

Colleges were offering significant financial support to students during that time. I joined a program for minority students that provided free books, a laptop, and tutoring.

The school also provided grant money.

That support helped cover my living expenses while I was in school.

Rent.

Food.

Gas.

The basic things that had once felt impossible to keep up with.

Because those things were taken care of, I was able to save the money I earned driving Lyft.

Little by little, ride by ride, I put money aside.

Eventually I had enough for a down payment on my own car.

It was not a luxury vehicle.

But it was mine.

No rental contract.

No repossession fear.

Just my own car.

And that meant independence.

Owning that car meant more to me than it might have meant to someone else. I knew what it felt like to lose a car. I knew what it felt like to sleep in one. I knew what it meant to depend on transportation just to survive. So having my own car again felt like a quiet victory. A small but meaningful piece of stability.

Around that same time, I started reconnecting with people in Nashville through a friend I had met years earlier at Jive Records.

Their stories about Nashville intrigued me.

A city filled with songwriters.

Musicians everywhere.

A place where music was not just an industry, but a culture.

I decided to go see it for myself.

I packed my car again and drove to Nashville.

And they were right.

The city truly lived and breathed music.

There was something about it that felt both grounded and creative. Less image driven than New York. Less performative than Los Angeles. It felt like a place where songs mattered.

But something unexpected happened while I was there.

A music executive I had met years earlier while pitching him a song reached out to me.

We had stayed in touch casually over time.

He mentioned something I did not expect.

A position in healthcare IT.

At first, I was shocked.

Honestly, I was a little offended.

I had spent years pursuing music. I was not looking to pivot into technology.

But he kept bringing it up over the next few weeks.

He talked about the pay.

The travel.

The opportunities.

At that time, I was delivering DoorDash and struggling to gain traction with music.

Eventually I thought, why not?

The company would train me on the system and cover travel expenses.

I decided to give it a chance.

They trained me on the software system and sent me to my first project in Utah.

I will never forget walking into that hospital on the first day.

My nerves were through the roof.

I realized very quickly that I did not know the system nearly as well as I hoped.

Many consultants in that situation would simply hide.

Some would sit in their cars during downtime.

Some would go back to their hotel rooms early.

But I made a decision.

I would show up.

Even if I did not know everything yet.

I introduced myself to the nurses and staff and told them honestly that I was still learning.

They could tell.

I am sure of it.

But something interesting happened.

They liked me.

They appreciated my honesty.

They appreciated my willingness to help however I could.

Instead of exposing me, they supported me.

They showed me little things about how the system worked. They answered my questions.

They guided me quietly.

I could have hidden like some consultants do.

But I wanted to learn.

The only way to learn was to stay present.

To stay humble.

To ask questions.

To show up.

That was the difference between me and some of the others. I did not want to pretend. I wanted to improve. I understood enough by then to know that ego blocks growth. Humility opens doors.

And that approach worked.

Project by project, I improved.

Before long I realized something surprising.

I actually enjoyed the work.

It required problem solving.

Communication.

Understanding how systems and people interact.

In many ways, it reminded me of music.

Different pieces working together to create harmony.

In November of 2020, I received an assignment in Houston, Texas.

It was my first time in the city.

What stood out to me immediately was seeing a young African American doctor confidently walking through the hospital wearing Jordans.

He was stylish.

Confident.

Successful.

For the first time, I saw professional success that looked like me.

That moment stayed with me.

It may have seemed small to someone else, but for me it was powerful. Representation matters. Seeing someone who looked like me occupying that level of professional space expanded my imagination in real time.

When I returned to Nashville, I could not stop thinking about Houston.

Eventually I reached out to a TikTok apartment locator and told her everything I was looking for.

She found the perfect place.

Once again, I packed my car.

And drove.

But this time it felt different.

I was not running.

I was stepping into something new.

A life that combined survival, growth, and possibility in ways I never expected.

And somehow, it all traced back to a five-minute Lyft ride with a stranger named Diane.

The woman who reminded me who I was when I had almost forgotten.

* * *

Live Music
Burlesque

10

From Scratch

In 2021, I did something I once believed would never be possible for me.

I graduated.

I earned my Associate's Degree in Political Science from Foothill College.

I did it quietly, without fanfare, without a large celebration or family gathered in an auditorium cheering my name. My graduation happened while my life was still in motion. I was living out of suitcases, navigating airports, hotel rooms, and unfamiliar cities. My classroom existed wherever my laptop happened to open that day.

Sometimes that meant logging into lectures from a quiet corner of a hotel room after a long workday. Sometimes it meant sitting in the passenger seat of a rental car, balancing my computer on my knees while trying to catch a discussion board deadline.

There were even moments when I found myself sitting near airport gates, headphones in, reviewing lecture notes while people rushed past me toward their flights.

My life still was not what most people would consider settled.

But something inside of me had finally stabilized.

For the first time in my life, I trusted myself.

That may sound small to someone else, but to me it was monumental. Trusting myself meant more than believing I could pass a class or turn in an assignment. It meant believing that I could build a life. It meant believing I could keep promises to myself. It meant believing that even if my path looked unconventional, it was still valid.

Graduating did not erase my past. It did not magically undo the years I spent feeling like I had been left behind or the moments when my path felt uncertain and chaotic. But it reframed my story.

Every setback.

Every detour.

Every moment where I had to rebuild my life from the ground up.

All of it had trained me for this moment.

I began to understand something important.

I was never behind.

I was being prepared.

After finishing at Foothill, I decided to continue my education and enrolled at the University of Houston Downtown to pursue my Bachelor's Degree in Political Science.

Once again, my life required balance.

I took my classes online while continuing to travel for work. My days became a constant juggling act between responsibilities. Flights. Project assignments. Hotel check-ins. Discussion boards. Papers. Exams. Deadlines that did not care what time zone I was in.

There were weeks when I felt like my entire life was moving in fast-forward.

Some mornings I woke up not even remembering which city I was in until I looked out the hotel window. The walls of hotels began to blur together. Beige bedding. Generic artwork. Ice machines down the hall. Tiny bottles of shampoo in the bathroom. My life existed in motion, and somehow I was trying to build an education inside of that movement.

But I stayed committed.

I stayed disciplined.

And slowly, semester by semester, I kept moving forward.

Still, there were moments when I questioned myself.

Why am I pushing this hard?

Why am I carrying so much at once?

Why not just settle for the progress I had already made?

But deep down, I knew this journey was about more than earning a degree.

This was about rewriting a story that had once been written for me.

A story that suggested I would never finish school.

A story that implied I had missed my chance.

A story that assumed my life would always exist in survival mode.

I was rewriting that story one class at a time.

And there was something almost sacred about that. Every paper I turned in. Every exam I studied for. Every discussion board I completed after a twelve-hour workday felt like an act of resistance against the version of my life that had once been decided for me.

My final semester nearly broke me.

I had enrolled in six classes while working twelve-hour shifts.

Six classes.

Twelve-hour workdays.

There were days when I ran completely on fumes.

Physically exhausted.

Mentally drained.

Emotionally stretched thin.

Some nights I stared at my laptop screen long after midnight trying to finish an assignment while my eyes struggled to stay open. Other nights I sat there thinking there was no way I was going to finish this. I remember feeling my body begging for rest while my mind kept pushing forward because I knew what was on the other side.

I doubted myself more than once.

But something stronger than doubt had already been built inside of me over the years.

Discipline.

Resilience.

Emotional mastery.

The same strength that helped me survive the darkest seasons of my life now carried me through the final stretch of school.

And somehow, by grace, grit, and determination, I crossed the finish line.

In 2023, I graduated with my Bachelor's Degree in Political Science from the University of Houston Downtown.

The girl who had not been enrolled in school after the sixth grade had done it.

That sentence still moves me.

Because it was never just about the diploma.

It was about reclaiming something that had been interrupted.

It was about proving to myself that a broken educational path did not mean a broken future.

But what made that moment even more powerful was not just the degree in my hand.

It was who stood there with me.

During that season of my life, something unexpected began happening.

I reconnected with my siblings.

For years we had been completely disconnected from one another. I did not know where they lived. I did not have their phone numbers. I did not know what their lives looked like.

But somehow, through social media, we found each other again.

At first it was awkward.

There were years of distance between us. Years of silence. Years of experiences we had lived separately. We had grown up in the same family but then been shaped by entirely different seasons of absence.

We did not know how to start the conversation.

But slowly we did.

A message here.

A reply there.

A little catching up.

A little testing the waters.

Eventually we exchanged phone numbers and began talking more regularly. Little by little, we started rebuilding what had been lost.

We were no longer children living under the same roof.

We were adults learning who each other had become.

There was grief in that. There was joy in that too. We could not recover the years, but we could choose what to do with the time we had now.

That reconnection meant more to me than I could explain.

Around that same time, I also reconnected with my father.

Our relationship had been distant for many years, but time has a way of softening things that once felt impossible. Sometimes distance clears enough space for people to meet each other again in a different way.

When my graduation approached, my father told me he wanted to come to Houston to be there.

My brother came too.

That day was special for many reasons.

It was the first time my father and my brother had ever met each other.

And it happened at my college graduation.

Watching the two of them stand there together was surreal. For so many years my life had felt fragmented, like pieces of my story existed in different places that could never fully come together.

But that day, for a moment, they did.

Seeing my father there.

Seeing my brother there.

Knowing they had come to support me.

It meant the world to me.

When I walked across that stage, I felt a wave of emotions I could barely contain.

Pride.

Relief.

Gratitude.

Healing.

I thought about the fourteen-year-old girl riding the bus to the library in Hartford because she did not have a school to attend.

I thought about the nights sleeping in my car.

The days of uncertainty.

The moments when I felt like my life had completely fallen apart.

And there I was.

Graduating.

With my family in the audience.

It was one of the most emotional moments of my life.

Not because everything had been perfectly restored.

But because enough had come back together for me to feel the beauty of the moment.

And yet, life has taught me that healing is not always linear.

After my graduation, my father slowly drifted from my life again.

There was no dramatic fallout.

No huge confrontation.

Just distance.

Silence.

Another fading.

I do not know exactly what he has been going through, and there are parts of that story that are not mine to tell. What I do know is that I no longer carry the same anger I once did.

I am at peace.

I have forgiven him.

And I have forgiven my mother too.

That forgiveness did not happen overnight. It came through time, prayer, maturity, and the understanding that carrying bitterness only keeps pain alive in your own body. Forgiveness did not mean pretending nothing happened. It meant refusing to let what happened own me forever.

I have learned that peace is sometimes more powerful than answers.

The plan after graduation was law school.

I took the LSAT and passed.

I began preparing applications, imagining courtrooms, advocacy, and a future rooted in justice. Law school made sense on paper. It aligned with my love of politics, my desire to understand systems, and the parts of me that had always been drawn to fairness and truth.

But while I was in the middle of that process, life presented me with something unexpected.

I received an offer for a full-time position with an organization that served underserved communities.

It was not glamorous.

It was not the path I had carefully mapped out.

But something about it felt right.

Maybe it was because, for the first time, opportunity and purpose were standing in the same doorway.

So I accepted.

And for the first time in my life, I experienced real stability.

A steady income.

A routine.

A sense of purpose that extended beyond survival.

I fell in love with the work.

I fell in love with helping people who were often overlooked by systems that were supposed to serve them. There was something grounding about being useful in a way that mattered, about helping real people navigate real problems, about knowing my work had tangible impact.

Houston began to feel like home.

Not temporary.

Not transitional.

Home.

That mattered to me more than I can express. For so much of my life, home had felt unstable. Temporary. Conditional. But in Houston, I began to feel rooted in a way I never had before.

Around the same time, music quietly found its way back into my life.

Not as a lifeline this time.

Not as an escape.

But as an extension of who I had become.

I released a new song simply because I wanted to express truth. I was not chasing validation anymore. I was creating because the music still lived inside me. It no longer had to rescue me. It could simply accompany me.

I met people organically.

Built relationships naturally.

For the first time in a long time, I was not running.

That was when a name kept coming up in conversations.

Exotic Pop.

People kept mentioning it.

You should collaborate with them.

You would be perfect for what they are doing.

Eventually I decided to reach out and set up a meeting.

What started as a simple conversation turned into something much bigger.

Together, we created Women Who Pop.

A platform designed to empower women business owners and female music artists.

A space where women could be visible.

Heard.

Celebrated.

What started as an idea quickly began growing.

Events.

Partnerships.

Community.

Energy.

As I looked around at what was forming, something became

clear to me.

Every version of me had led here.

The girl who was forced out of school.

The young woman chasing music in New York.

The alter ego who learned confidence through performance.

The woman sleeping in her car learning humility.

The student fighting for education.

The professional finding stability.

The artist rediscovering her voice.

The leader creating space for others.

None of it had been wasted.

That realization changed the way I looked at my life. The pain had not been pointless. The confusion had not been empty. Even the delays had direction in them. Every chapter had built something in me that I would eventually need.

Looking back over my life now, I can clearly see God's hand guiding every step, even when I believed I was completely lost.

Even when I thought I was starting over again.

I was never starting over.

I was building.

From scratch.

Transformation did not happen overnight.

It happened in layers.

In choices.

In moments where I chose discipline over despair.

Faith over fear.

Growth over comfort.

Emotional mastery over emotional chaos.

I learned something powerful along the way.

When you master your emotions, you master your direction.

When you master your direction, you master your future.

I built this life without a blueprint.

Without a safety net.

Without guarantees.

Only belief.

Consistency.

And obedience to the next step.

Brick by brick.

Lesson by lesson.

Season by season.

And if there is one thing I know for sure now, it is this.

You do not need a perfect beginning to build a powerful life.

You do not need permission to transform.

You do not need to have everything figured out.

You just need the courage to begin.

From scratch.

* * *

11

Epilogue

If you had met me years ago, sleeping in the backseat of my car in a quiet parking lot somewhere in California, you probably would not have believed where my life would eventually land.

Back then my world felt small.

Uncertain.

Temporary.

Every day felt like survival. Every decision felt like a gamble. I was constantly trying to rebuild pieces of a life that had fallen apart more than once.

What I did not understand at the time was that those seasons were shaping something inside me that I would eventually need.

Resilience.

Clarity.

Faith.

And most importantly, emotional mastery.

The truth is, transformation rarely looks the way we imagine it will.

We often think transformation means one big breakthrough moment. One life-changing opportunity. One perfect decision that suddenly turns everything around.

But that is not how my life unfolded.

My transformation happened slowly.

Quietly.

Layer by layer.

It happened in moments when I chose discipline over despair.

It happened when I chose growth over comfort.

It happened when I chose to keep going even when nothing around me suggested that success was guaranteed.

Looking back now, I realize that the most powerful shifts in my life happened when I stopped trying to force a specific outcome and instead focused on becoming the kind of person who could handle whatever came next.

That shift changed everything.

Today my life looks very different from the one I once imagined.

I live in Houston, Texas, a city that welcomed me at a time when I was finally ready for stability. My career in healthcare technology allows me to help organizations serve communities that are often overlooked by systems that were designed to support them.

The work is meaningful.

It grounds me.

It reminds me that purpose does not always arrive in the form we expect.

Music is still part of my life, but it exists in a different way now.

It is no longer the thing I depend on to rescue me from my circumstances.

It is something I return to when I want to express truth.

When I create music now, it comes from a place of peace rather than desperation. It is no longer about chasing validation or proving something to the world. It is about honoring the part of myself that has always found language through melody.

The woman I once called Etta Mae still lives inside me.

She taught me confidence.

She taught me presence.

She taught me how to take up space in rooms that once made me feel invisible.

But today I understand that Etta Mae was never meant to replace Shauna.

She was meant to protect her.

She gave me armor during seasons when I needed strength to survive environments that demanded performance, image, and resilience.

But eventually I had to learn how to live without armor.

That required a different kind of courage.

The courage to be whole.

Another unexpected chapter of my life emerged through collaboration.

What started as a simple conversation eventually became **Women Who Pop**, a platform designed to empower women business owners and female artists. Through events, partnerships, and community building, we created spaces where women could show up fully as themselves.

Women Who Pop is not just about music or entrepreneurship.

It is about visibility.

It is about reminding women that their ideas, their voices, and their creativity deserve space.

Watching that platform grow has been one of the most fulfilling experiences of my life.

Because every time I see a woman step forward with confidence, I see a reflection of the girl I once was.

The girl who felt unseen.

The girl who wondered if she would ever find her place in the world.

My personal brand, **Homemade Cake**, was born from that same philosophy.

The idea is simple.

You are the cake you bake yourself.

Transformation is not something handed to you by outside validation.

It is something you build through your choices, your discipline, and your willingness to evolve.

Every ingredient matters.

Every season matters.

Even the painful ones.

Especially the painful ones.

Because those seasons shape the texture of who you become.

Another blessing that returned to my life has been family.

For many years I lived with the quiet grief of separation from my siblings. We had grown up together but had been pulled apart by circumstances that none of us fully understood at the time.

Through social media and small moments of courage, we eventually found our way back to one another.

The conversations were awkward at first.

There were years of silence between us.

Years of experiences we had lived separately.

But slowly we began rebuilding something that had once felt impossible to restore.

Today we continue to grow that relationship.

Not as children trying to survive the same household.

But as adults learning who each other has become.

I also reconnected with my father in ways that once felt unimaginable.

Watching him meet my brother for the first time at my college graduation was one of the most emotional moments of my life.

It reminded me that healing does not always happen all at once.

Sometimes it happens quietly.

In moments where people simply show up.

My life today is not perfect.

But it is whole.

And that is something I once believed might never happen.

If there is one thing I want readers to understand from my story, it is this.

You do not need a perfect beginning to build a powerful life.

Your circumstances may delay you.

They may challenge you.

They may even break parts of you.

But they do not get the final say over who you become.

The final say belongs to the choices you make after everything falls apart.

I built my life without a blueprint.

Without a safety net.

Without guarantees.

Only belief.

Consistency.

Faith.

And the willingness to start again whenever necessary.

Brick by brick.

Lesson by lesson.

Season by season.

So if you are reading this and your life feels uncertain...

If you feel like you are starting over again...

If you feel like your dreams have been delayed beyond repair...

I want you to know something.

You are not starting over.

You are building.

From scratch.

About the Author

Shauna Young is a writer, musician, entrepreneur, and technology professional whose life journey reflects resilience, reinvention, and transformation. After leaving formal schooling at a young age, she later earned her GED and went on to receive both an Associate's Degree and a Bachelor's Degree in Political Science.

Her career spans music, healthcare technology, and community empowerment. Shauna has worked in the healthcare industry supporting hospitals and clinics with electronic health record systems while continuing to nurture her passion for music, storytelling, and creative expression.

She is the founder of Homemade Cake, a lifestyle brand built around the message of personal transformation and self-creation. Through Homemade Cake, Shauna encourages women to embrace growth, discipline, and the power of rebuilding their lives on their own terms.

Shauna is also the co-founder of Women Who Pop, a platform created to uplift and empower women entrepreneurs and female artists through events, collaboration, and community.

The Homemade Transformation is her debut book, sharing the deeply personal story of overcoming adversity, rediscovering purpose, and building a life from scratch.

Shauna currently lives in Houston, Texas, where she continues to create, inspire, and encourage others to pursue transformation in every area of their lives.

You can connect with me on:

https://www.homemadecakeapparel.com

https://www.facebook.com/Yoshauna

www.ingramcontent.com/pod-product-compliance
Ingram Content Group UK Ltd.
Pitfield, Milton Keynes, MK11 3LW, UK
UKHW041046300726
14061UKWH00008BA/105